Ghost Stories, Urban Legends, &
Hidden Places in Ontario, Canada

Part 1

Written by Deborah Schneider-Gagné

Cover art by Austin Gagné

Photography by Colleen J. Cairney and
Deborah Schneider-Gagné

Research Assistance by Kane Gagné

Book Cover Art by Austin Gagné

Photography by Deborah Schneider-Gagné and Colleen J. Cairney

Research Assistance by Kane Gagné

First edition 2024

Table of Contents

In memory of Bernard J. Gagné

1

Introduction

Since childhood, I've been fascinated by ghost stories, abandoned sites, and urban legends. Many historic buildings echo tales of the past, instilling a sense of adventure and discovery at a young age. I recall hearing all sorts of interesting tales: local legends and stories of hauntings, old roads with apparitions, and suspicious houses abandoned by their owners, sometimes due to paranormal sightings and unusual, or downright frightening activities. In some stories, people vacated villages due to a closed lumber mill or natural catastrophe. Many of these stories are like folklore and fairy tales, woven as urban legends and strange stories passed down from one generation to the next.

As a child, I often thought about these stories and places. They kept me up at night pondering how true they were. I was also intrigued. If these accounts were real, what type of phenomena were causing them? Did ghosts, demons, hallucinations, or bizarre twists in space and time produce these effects or apparitions? Eventually, I grew more skeptical of these tales, yet I always wanted to read and learn more about them. Despite encountering a few experiences later in my teens and throughout adulthood, I often leaned towards finding a logical explanation, though some incidents remained mysterious. It wasn't until later that I began to attend ghost walks and discuss some of the region's well-known urban legends that I became drawn to visit more sites and see for myself.

As a parent, I enjoy storytelling, and my kids soon learned of a few haunting tales. We didn't talk about it extensively at first, but they began to share their interest over time. Like most kids, they developed a natural curiosity to find out more. Something is exciting about discovering mysteries and the unknown, opening a world of imagination and creativity. Touring historic sites, castles, tunnels, and a lighthouse and traveling with a keen eye for the unusual grew into a unique hobby. The thrill of finding a new or forgotten place, the ruins of a ghost town, or the preserved house of a famous politician from a century ago were journeys across time and into a world that was different from now yet remained present still.

When you visit a place infamous for its urban legend or ghost tales, you'll likely hear some tips on exploring them. Some sites are easy to find, well-documented, and mapped. In contrast, others are obscure, requiring significant research and "hunting" when traditional maps and GPS coordinates don't always yield accurate results. After years of following tour guides and historical tales in several Southern Ontario regions, we expanded our exploration and took our own trips. From the Gibraltar Lighthouse on Toronto Island and hidden tunnels in Niagara Region to the Hermitage ruins left from over a century ago and haunted roads, we've found and continue to search for many unique and exciting places, including our trek for the perfect ghost town!

In 2020, we explored more obscure and hidden sites we had yet to see. As usual, we took pictures and researched a lot of information to understand these places many years ago. These visits prompted me to include our previous experiences touring historical sites, ghost towns, and places with a history of paranormal activity. Reading online blog posts and photos was fun, though taking a more in-depth approach to documenting and sharing our experiences became a primary focus. We decided a book would be the logical next step and provide a new way to discover these fascinating places locally, in and around Southern Ontario.

This book is our first report on our findings, combined with some history, tales, and fun facts we uncovered along the way. I hope you enjoy the book and that it inspires you to begin exploring! The goal of this book is to ignite further interest in these sites' histories, learn more about little-known places, and to find more hidden gems around Southern Ontario.

1.
The Screaming Tunnel, Niagara Region (Niagara-on-the-lake, Ontario)

A view of the Screaming Tunnel as of July 2020 from the Bruce Grey trail. On the opposite side is Warner Road (D. Schneider-Gagné)

The Screaming Tunnel is among Niagara's oldest and most infamous legends. We initially read about the Screaming Tunnel from online articles, documented video footage, and reports from paranormal investigators in and around the Greater Toronto Area, Niagara Region, and Hamilton. If you search YouTube videos and online blogs, you'll find fascinating videos and reports of what lurks inside and around this scary tunnel. The site is located along the Bruce Grey hiking trail, creating a scenic trip with many natural wonders to discover and enjoy. It's surprisingly easy to find, located just off Warner Road, not far from the town of Thorold, and Niagara Falls. We spent the weekend enjoying a ghost tour in Niagara-on-the-lake and some hiking outdoors, then we decided to add this spot to our itinerary.

The History of the Screaming Tunnel

The tunnel was constructed as early as 1900 to create a drainage system to prevent flooding from impacting the railway tracks above. It also provided an easy route for residents, farmers, and hikers to travel and bypass the trains in later years. The tunnel was built with limestone bricks, which are porous and contain a lot of moisture, moss, and plant life, giving the site an eerie atmosphere. Many visitors to the tunnel reported a distinct smell. This odour is attributed to the build up of moisture and plant life that grows in and around the tunnel.

Today, the tunnel runs beneath railway tracks that provide train service between Toronto and New York City, making many stops along this corridor. It was a convenient drainage system, giving farmers a safe, and more efficient passage. The tunnel's interior extends to 125 feet in length, and 16 feet in height.

The Tunnel's Feature in a Famous Movie and on TV Shows

In 1982, the tunnel was part of a climactic scene in David Cronenberg's film The Dead Zone. The Screaming Tunnel was also featured in a short dramatization, in an episode from Creepy Canada, about the site's urban legend and reported hauntings.

The interior of the tunnel, from the passage facing Warner Road, July 2020 (D. Schneider-Gagné)

The Legend of the Screaming Tunnel, in Three Versions

The origin of the Screaming Tunnel's story is debatable, as there are no physical recordings or reports of the girl who allegedly disappeared and was then found in the tunnel. Over the past century, numerous versions of the story endured, with each tale ending with the girl's tragic death.

In one version, the girl escapes from her home due to a fire set by an oil lamp. It's unclear whether her parents survived or if she had any siblings or family with her. As she ran from her home, wearing a nightgown engulfed in flames, she quickly remembered the tunnel, well known for its damp conditions and interior flooding, and hoped to extinguish the fire and survive. As the girl reached the entrance to the tunnel, she was overcome by her injuries, collapsed, barely making it inside, where she took her last breath.

Another popular version of this story is more sinister and alleged that the same girl was a victim of abuse and murder. In this tale, her father became enraged when he learned of his wife's plan to leave him and take their daughter due to alcoholism and physical abuse. The mother had begun divorce proceedings, but her husband wasn't about to let them leave and deliberately set the house on fire. When the girl escaped, making her way to the tunnel, her father followed her with a can of kerosene and matches. Then, horrifically, he doused her in the flammable liquid, and set her on fire, just as they approached the tunnel's center. The flames would not extinguish despite the wet conditions, and the girl tragically died.

Other versions of this story involve people who lived in the village and knew the young girl. The third version of this legend accused a local shop owner of abusing and murdering the girl, then discarding her remains inside or near the tunnel. Over a century, these three main versions have been told and then revised so that there are further variations and added details. While the horrific, tragic tale changes drastically, each version of the tale ends the same and involves the death of a young girl.

Graffiti just outside of the Screaming Tunnel, July 2020 (D. Schneider-Gagné)

Paranormal Sightings and Ghost Stories

There are many tales of sightings and strange activity in the Screaming Tunnel, making it one of the most famous urban legends in the region. If you inquire with locals and people familiar with the legend, the most common version of the story claims that the girl was a victim of a violent crime resulting in her death. It is alleged that her body was burned and left in the center of the tunnel. This spot is rumoured to be where most (if not all) paranormal sightings and experiences occur. Despite variations to this tale, the reported hauntings involve the girl's screams, which occur around midnight or early morning.

According to the legend, if you visit the tunnel at midnight or between two and three o'clock in the morning, you're most likely to experience the phenomenon. You must light a match in the tunnel's center using wooden matches, striking one against the box, and you will hear the girl's screams. The flame will go out, and further attempts to light a second or third match will extinguish.

There are also reports of seeing apparitions of the girl inside the tunnel, screaming. In other instances, the screams are disembodied and heard throughout the interior. An apparition of a man, just outside or within the tunnel entrance, has also been reported, carrying a lantern. This sighting resembles what many people think is the girl's father, who is moving toward the center of the structure. Many visitors experience a breeze or cold air inside the tunnel, attributed to its damp interior and cooler temperature.

Inside the Screaming Tunnel, July 2020 (D. Schneider-Gagné)

Our Visit to the Screaming Tunnel in July 2020

On a trip to Niagara-on-the-lake, we enjoyed sightseeing in the historic downtown on our first night. The next day, we ventured into the outskirts to find the Screaming Tunnel. It was early in the evening, and just hours before our hike, we spotted funnel clouds near Thorold. There had been a storm warning earlier, which had since passed. The turbulent winds could be seen from our hotel room window, as we were located close to Thorold, and just next to Niagara-on-the-Lake. The dark, ominous clouds and warm winds set the mood for an exciting night.

We found the tunnel quickly, located just off Warner Road. It's visible from the road and easily seen as a well-known regional landmark on street-view maps. It was still light outdoors, though the sun quickly set as we explored the area in and around the tunnel.

We entered from the side facing the street as we approached the Screaming Tunnel. It's set in, so you have to walk several meters to reach it, and there are lots of trees and bushes around the entrance. If you visit in the spring or after a rainfall, you'll notice a lot of mud and slippery conditions in and around the structure.

The interior is damp, as there is a lot of moisture and moss on the stones, which creates a strong odour you pass from one end of the tunnel to the other. Exiting through the opposite side, you will find it's part of the Bruce Grey Trail, which leads through a wooded area with access to meadows and fields nearby. As we explored this area until night, we found many fireflies and a few frogs along the trail. Eventually, we made our way back through the tunnel, returning to Warren Road and then, to the hotel.

How was our encounter with the Screaming Tunnel? It was a creepy experience, but this was primarily due to our prior knowledge of its legendary status in the Niagara Region, the damp, eerie visuals of the limestone interior, and the expectations of our visit. While we hoped to find something unusual or unexplainable, nothing happened. We left around ten o'clock at night and didn't attempt to light a wooden match at midnight. Our visit to this spot was fun, and I recommend making the trip if you are in the area.

2.

The Blue Ghost Tunnel, Niagara Region (Thornton, Ontario)

The exterior of the Merritton Tunnel at night, November 2020 (D. Schneider-Gagné)

One of the most infamous sites for urban legends and ghost stories in the Niagara Region is the Blue Ghost Tunnel. It's also known as the Merritton Tunnel. Unlike the Screaming Tunnel, this abandoned site requires a sense of adventure and a bit of hiking to find its exact location. If you search for this spot using online maps, you'll notice it's between Thorold and Niagara-on-the-Lake. It isn't easily accessible from the main road, as it's hidden just off a closed road, which is also abandoned. It runs along the Welland Canal and several locks, which you can see from a nearby bridge on Glendale Avenue.

You'll notice an unused or closed-off street called Seaway Haulage Road when you pass over the Glendale Avenue Bridge. This road initially starts from Glendale Avenue, turning left, forming a loop that travels above, then below the same road, beneath a bridge. It continues as Seaway Haulage Road, following a landscape of forested areas, concrete ruins, a small bridge, and alongside one of the local canals. The tunnel is difficult to see or access directly from the closed road, though a quick trek through a grassy, forested area will lead you to this unique site.

A closer look at the tunnel, with the entrance sealed off for safety precautions, November 2020 (D. Schneider-Gagné)

The History of the Blue Ghost Tunnel

The Merritton Tunnel was built around the same time as the wooden locks were constructed, during the opening of the Welland Canal system. The first canal was opened in 1829, followed by the second and third locks. While the second lock was completed around 1845, the third lock wasn't built until 1872, requiring larger locks that ran deeper than the first two. Further modifications were needed when it was determined that the Grand Trunk Railway would benefit from a shorter route across the canal. So, a tunnel was constructed between 1875 and 1876 to provide a passageway.

The nearby Welland Canal system, July 2020 (D. Schneider-Gagné)

When the railway tunnel was built, it was formally named the Merritton Tunnel after William Merrit, who developed the plan to join Lake Erie and Lake Ontario with a canal system in the early 1800s. Constructed of Queenston Limestone, the tunnel measures a distance of just over 700 feet. While the tunnel was open for approximately fifty years, it was closed and abandoned in 1915. During the construction and use of the tunnel in the late nineteenth century, several tragic events occurred, which are believed to haunt this site.

The interior of the Blue Ghost Tunnel as seen through the barred entrance with a flashlight, November 2020 (D. Schneider-Gagné)

The Legend of the Blue Ghost Tunnel

Several tragic tales plague the historic tunnel. During the bridge and tunnel construction, it is believed that many people were seriously injured, and that several deaths occurred, including child laborers and a dog. A young Irish boy died from a large rock, crushing him in or around the structure. In 1903, two trains collided on the tracks just above the tunnel, instantly killing a firefighter aboard one of the trains. According to this legend, the man's remains were a grisly find, as they were intertwined with the locomotives.

The infamous tunnel is between locks 18 and 19, where the third Welland Canal was previously located. Since its construction, the tunnel has been operational from the late 1800s until its closure in 1915. While the tunnel was open during this 50 to - 60-year period, it was not used regularly due to poor maintenance and structural issues. These circumstances only worsened when the Grand Trunk Railway Company took over the site from the Great Western Railway Company. According to historical records, the single-track railway design was quickly replaced with a double-track swing bridge installed. By 1930, the tunnel was closed.

Due to the numerous tragedies and fatalities at the site, the Blue Ghost Tunnel is considered one of the most haunted locations in Southern Ontario. It's also one of the most popular abandoned sites in the Niagara Region.

Paranormal Sightings and Ghost Stories

The Merritton Tunnel was renamed the Blue Ghost Tunnel because of the interior's eerie appearance, described as having a blue "ghostly" light by a paranormal investigator who discovered the abandoned site years ago. The eerie glow seemed to float and resemble an entity or apparition. Since its early discovery, there have been reports of paranormal sightings and unusual experiences in the tunnel and surrounding area.

Many people believe that the ghosts or spirits of individuals who tragically died at the site continue to haunt this place today. It has become a popular spot for ghost tours, paranormal investigators, and individuals with a sense of adventure and interest in abandoned urban sites. Some ghost tour guides and individual explorers have reported strange flashing lights inside the tunnel or an apparition of a dog or a person, which suddenly disappears, leaving behind the unsettling sound of dripping.

While many of the visitors to the Merritton Tunnel reported unusual lighting, a constant dripping sound, and sightings of apparitions or strange phenomena, many of these experiences are attributed to the tunnel's damp and muddy interior, which is unstable and continuously leaking. The entrance to the tunnel, on the side where it's accessible, is often closed or sealed off with a gate to prevent curious visitors from trekking through the unstable interior. Occasionally, you may find the bolted entrance broken, then quickly repaired to prevent accidents.

Our Visit to the Blue Ghost Tunnel in November 2020

When you venture off Seaway Haulage Road, conveniently paved, a narrow, dirt, and grassy path leads you to the Blue Ghost Tunnel. We visited in mid-November on an unusually warm day, though some areas were slippery. These conditions are prevalent during spring and autumn or after a major rainfall. The terrain is bumpy, requiring a bit of caution to navigate this area. When we arrived at the tunnel, it was sealed off to prevent injury, and water leaked continuously from the ceiling.

We began our hike in the late afternoon, and it was dark by the time we found the tunnel. This part of the structure is the west side entrance, which is sealed off with a door and metal bars, though it has been previously broken or unlocked, only to be closed off again. If you shine a flashlight or the light from your phone or camera through the barred entrance, you'll catch a decent glimpse inside the tunnel. The wet, muddy ground, uneven surface, and constant dripping water from above would be considered unsafe.

The tunnel is periodically flooded, creating a dangerous environment for any explorer in or around the site. We noticed the grassy patches and mud around the entrance were slippery, so it was best to approach slowly and carefully, even if you're equipped with rubber boots and hiking gear.

The east entrance is submerged in water, and parts are flooded beneath the Wellington Canal, which would be impossible to access, even with scuba equipment. The atmosphere around the west tunnel entrance was damp, and it did feel creepy and uninviting. We spent about half an hour exploring the area in and around the tunnel, though we did not experience paranormal occurrences or eerie sightings.

3.

Old Finch Avenue (Scarborough, Ontario)

Old Finch Avenue on a cloudy evening in November 2021 (D. Schneider-Gagné)

Old Finch Avenue is a historic road in Scarborough, in the northeast district of Toronto. It's well-known for its urban legends and reported hauntings. It's located near the Malvern neighbourhood, which has become a popular place for teenagers to explore, especially at night, when there are reported sightings of a girl who met a tragic end at the bridge. Old Finch Avenue is a short distance from the Toronto Zoo and includes a small bridge where the street narrows so that only one vehicle can safely pass at a time.

The History of Old Finch Avenue and the Bailey Bridge

The Old Finch Bridge was constructed by the Canadian Army and opened in late 1954. The entire process took only several days, using components from an older bridge at the Ontario Hydro-Electric Power Commission, which was destroyed by Hurricane Hazel that same year. It was a simple, sturdy structure built to accommodate one lane of traffic, which meant oncoming cars would need to slow down when approaching the bridge to ensure a clear path before proceeding. This bridge is what distinguishes Old Finch Avenue as unique; it provides a passage across the Rouge River and appears to separate the residential neighbourhood from the forested area just outside the city's borders. It's considered a historic landmark, and a plaque is located next to the bridge, commemorating the efforts involved with its construction.

Also known as a Bailey Bridge, the Old Finch Avenue bridge was one of several built following Hurricane Hazel, which either severely damaged or destroyed several bridges around the City of Scarborough, which has since amalgamated to become part of Toronto. It is a functioning part of the road, with traffic lights, making it easier to spot from a distance.

The Legend of the Birthday Girl and the School Bus Accident

The infamous road and its narrow bridge are considered one of the most haunted spots in the city. One popular tale about the Old Finch structure, close to Morningside Avenue, is about a girl brutally murdered on the bridge on her birthday. While this story has travelled from one generation to the next as a source of the unusual activity occurring in and around the bridge, there are no reports from newspapers, the police, or evidence that the murder ever occurred.

Another legend says that train tracks crossing Old Finch are haunted by the ghosts of children killed in a school bus accident in the 1970s. If you park your car on the tracks and shut off the engine, your car will be suddenly "pushed" off the tracks to safety, and you'll see the hand prints of the dead children all over your car.

Our view of Old Finch Avenue on the way to the bridge, November 2021 (D. Schneider-Gagné)

Reports of Hauntings and Unusual Activity

Old Finch Avenue is a well-known spot in the neighbourhood of Malvern that is said to be haunted by several ghosts. Many of the reported hauntings along the bridge are attributed to the young girl, Candy, who is believed to have been walking home from her birthday party when she met her unfortunate fate.

Over the years, it's become a popular destination for paranormal investigators, who often visit a nearby cemetery and historic church. According to the legend of Old Finch Avenue, anyone walking across the bridge at night may hear the disembodied screams of a young girl. If you sing Happy Birthday or call out to the girl by name, you'll hear the high-pitched screams of terror. In some tales, it is suggested that standing on the bridge, in the center, when the sky is darkest and everything is quiet, is when you'll most likely experience the paranormal. It is at this time you will be able to hear the girl's screams, and if you sing, the spirit of Candy will be summoned and respond.

Other experiences have been reported involving the sound of footsteps following closely behind as pedestrians approach or cross the bridge, only to find no one there when they turn around. Some people have experienced trouble with their vehicle as they drive towards the bridge, where the car either breaks down or other issues arise suddenly and without explanation. Some people have also claimed to hear voices and screams originating from a nearby cemetery, and a set of train tracks nearby are also reported to cause parked vehicles to be pushed or moved if stopped on or close to the tracks.

View of the Old Finch Bridge at night, November 2021 (D. Schneider-Gagné)

Our Visit to Old Finch Avenue

We visited the historic bridge and road in mid-November 2021. The road stretches from Old Finch Avenue down Sewells Road, with turns onto another section of Old Finch, which leads to the bridge. It's located in the Morningside Heights neighbourhood. It winds through a rural-like area surrounded by forests, leading towards the Toronto Zoo and the Rouge National Urban Park, a scenic place popular for year-round hiking and panoramic views. We walked down Old Finch Avenue towards the bridge when we arrived near the site. The residential dwellings abruptly end when you turn down Sewell Road, where we found fenced-off areas sectioning off trees, park areas, and minimal light, as there were no traffic or street lights on this stretch of road.

Carefully following the road in the dusk, we periodically checked our location and proximity to the bridge, which only took roughly ten minutes to find. Since there were no sidewalks, we followed the grassy shoulder of the road slowly until we found the bridge. Aside from vehicles traveling through this area, the atmosphere felt a little creepy, and the cold, rainy weather definitely contributed to this experience. Once we reached the bridge, the only light sources were the single set of traffic lights just before the bridge and our smartphone flashlights.

As we crossed the bridge, it became imminent that we watch closely for vehicles, as there would be little or no room to stand on the bridge as a vehicle passed by. While we didn't experience any unusual activity in the area or on the bridge, we found the quiet between cars unsettling, especially in the dark. The parking space surrounding the road and the bridge have also been popular locations for parties and adventurous teenagers, so any screams or noises heard from previous visitors may have originated from a partygoer and not the spirit or energy of the birthday girl, rumoured to haunt the place.

4.

Gibraltar Lighthouse (Toronto Island, Ontario)

A photo of the historic Gilbratar Lighthouse, May 2021 (D. Schneider-Gagné)

One of Toronto's oldest and most haunted buildings is the Gibraltar Point Lighthouse, located on the south part of Center Island. It's one of the Toronto islands, located between Hanlan's Point and Ward's Island. The lighthouse was completed in 1808, where it remains today, just a short walk from the island's south shore, which faces the United States across Lake Ontario. At the time of its construction, Toronto was called the Town of York. Lieutenant Governor John Graves Simcoe chose the lighthouse location when he decided that Toronto would become the military center of southern Ontario, called Upper Canada at that time. One of the reasons for the lighthouse's placement was its opposing yet proximity to Fort York, on the city's mainland, towards the shore.

View from the top of the lighthouse, May 2014 (D. Schneider-Gagné)

Before the lighthouse and other structures on the Toronto Islands, the Indigenous people lived on and used the islands, or Mnisiing, to seek peace and recreation. They called the islands Hiawatha's Island or Aiionwatha.

The History of the Gibraltar Lighthouse: 1793 to Today

When the original lighthouse was built in 1793, it stood just fifty-two feet high, with a lantern, overlooking the western entrance to the harbour. It was constructed with large stones, which were transported by vessel to the island. The base consisted of six-foot-thick walls and a hexagon-shaped structure. As the lighthouse gradually narrowed towards the top, the walls decreased to a thickness of four feet.

Interior of the Gibraltar Lighthouse, May 2014 (D. Schneider-Gagné)

One of the advantages of building the Gibraltar Lighthouse was the safety it provided to vessels traveling at night. Just outside the lantern room, a flag was raised to signal nearby Fort York, on the mainland, of any approaching ships. The iconic lighthouse was active during the War of 1812, and it was the first building ships and fleets nearing the peninsula would see as they approached the shore.

Throughout the nineteenth century, several modifications were made to the Gibraltar Lighthouse. It was raised to a height of sixty-four feet, with additional stonework, in 1832, which resulted in a total of eighty-two feet from the ground to the top of the vane. The structure's interior consisted of a spiral staircase leading up to a hexagon-shaped gallery with a wooden lantern inside a cage. The lamp's visibility stretched up to seven miles and burned through roughly two hundred gallons of sperm whale oil every year.

The fuel source was replaced with coal in the mid-1860s - a more cost-effective option. Then, in 1878, a lightning rod was installed at the top of the lighthouse tower, constructed of steel, which averted a disaster when lightning struck the following year, in 1879. It was fortunate timing, as, without the rod, the tower could have easily been destroyed. The lamp was modified for electricity after the turn of the century and later to modernize and protect the structure. In the early 1960s, the lighthouse's operations were taken over by the city's parks department, and during this time, additional renovations were completed.

A rare visit inside the top of the Gilbraltar Lighthouse, May 2014 (D. Schneider-Gagné)

Today, the lighthouse is well preserved, and the interior is rarely accessible and opened only during the occasional tour. Since its decommissioning in the 1950s and the receding of Lake Ontario, the lighthouse is set inland approximately one hundred feet from the shoreline, a short walking distance from the nearby beach and Hanlan's Point. It's a hidden gem that attracts curious visitors to the Toronto Islands yearly, offering picturesque photographs and a few unique ghost stories.

The Infamous Hauntings and Story of the Lighthouse Keeper

The entrance into the lighthouse, May 2014 (D. Schneider-Gagné)

Years ago, I watched a dramatization of the infamous story of J.P. Radenmuller, the first lighthouse keeper, on a television show called Creepy Canada. He was known to regular visitors and soldiers in the area until he disappeared unexpectedly. This is also well-documented in several articles, blogs, and videos. While the mysterious disappearance occurred in 1815, it wasn't until decades later that human bones were found near the lighthouse, including a jaw bone and a makeshift coffin, which were suspected to be the remains of Radenmuller.

Several variations in the story of his death center around a local bootlegging operation and a deal he made with local soldiers. In one story, the lighthouse keeper closed his liquor-making operation, his well-known side business, early one evening. This led to a violent confrontation with two soldiers, which resulted in his murder. In another version, J.P. Radenmuller decided to dilute a batch of liquor before selling it to the soldiers. When they discovered this shady dealing, they plotted to seek revenge.

It is not confirmed how the lighthouse keeper was killed. The soldiers may have crept into the lighthouse, tip-toeing up the staircase to confront him. Then, they threw him down the sprial steps to an early grave. It was also suspected that a vicious stabbing with an axe led to the brutal end of the lighthouse keeper. While there was considerable variation in stories and theories about Radenmuller's disappearance and his suspected murder, no one was convicted despite several soldiers standing trial. The case went cold and remains unsolved today.

Many people have reported sightings of the lighthouse keeper in various forms. His spirit is believed to haunt the lighthouse and the nearby grounds, a place John Paul Radenmuller called home in the early 1800s. Tales of paranormal activity range from unusual sounds and lights to apparitions of a man walking around the lighthouse, sometimes as a silhouette or as a grotesque, bloodied version of his remains, reanimated. It's more common to experience an encounter after dark, though the lighthouse is a popular site to visit during the day.

Our Visit to the Lighthouse

I've often marveled at the lighthouse during many visits to Toronto Island, either on my bicycle, after spending the day at the Center Island theme park with my kids, or enjoying a leisurely walk in autumn. During one annual Doors Open tour, the lighthouse was unlocked and accessible to the public for a few hours. We stood in line to enter the two-hundred-year-old building, climbing the staircase to the lamp, where you could enjoy a different perspective of the city's skyline to the north of the island and the Lake leading towards the United States to the south.

My kids enjoyed the tale of the lighthouse keeper and of hauntings in and around the building. On one cloudy afternoon, during a picnic beside the lighthouse, I described some of the stories of sightings, including apparitions of John Paul Radenmuller. At that moment, a man suddenly appeared around one side of the structure, causing all of us to jump. He was also interested in the lighthouse's dark history and reports of unusual activity over the past two centuries. The timing was perfect for the ultimate jump-scare, as we had just talked about visuals of the legendary lighthouse keeper just as the man appeared. This unique site continues to fascinate many due to the mysterious disappearance of the lighthouse keeper, its history, and numerous reports of hauntings.

5.

Coopers Falls, Ghost Town (Muskoka Region, Ontario)

Remnants of the once thriving Cooper's Falls, near Washago, Ontario, May 2021 (D. Schneider-Gagné)

Ontario has hundreds of ghost towns and forgotten communities from the mid-1800s until the 1900s. Coopers Falls is just outside of Washago, a small town north of Orillia. In May 2021, I enjoyed a scenic hike to this ghost town, which originally boasted a population of several hundred people, including a lumber mill, a general store, a church, and several shops. This scenic location, near the Black River, is home to approximately ten residents.

Photo of the Black River in Coopers Falls, May 2021 (D. Schneider-Gagné)

The History of Coopers Falls

Thomas and Emma Cooper settled in this tiny but vibrant town in the mid to late 1870s. The couple immigrated from England, where their families and community ostracised them. Emma, born into a wealthy family, married Thomas, the son of a local butcher, who was considered of a lower socio-economic status. Following their marriage, they decided to escape the clutches of a rigid society and traveled to Ontario, Canada. In the 1860s, they moved with their children, initially settling in Toronto. Later, the young family embarked further north, by boat and train, to establish their community.

Gradually, Thomas and Emma Cooper built a village within the untamed land where food and resources were scarce. There was little to no help and no close neighbours, and wild animals, including wolves, roamed regularly. Fishing, hunting, and rationing food portions were a way of life for the family until they began to attract new people to join their community by building a log cabin schoolhouse. As the couple established a village over time, they built a new house, general store, church, post office, and several other buildings alongside the Black River waterfall. As immigration soared in the area, a sawmill and lumber business began to attract new residents to the area, who set up camp.

By the late 1870s and 1880s, Coopers Falls grew into a vibrant town of several hundred, with a thriving lumber industry, a cheese factory, a blacksmith, a schoolhouse, and two churches (Anglican and Methodist). This sustainable village was profitable for the Coopers, who enjoyed steady business, regular delivery of supplies, and connections to nearby towns and industries. In the early 1900s, improvements to road conditions and access and the construction of two nearby railway stations, Severn Bridge and Washago, made it easy to visit and travel through town. This progress was further enhanced with telephones in the early 1910s and electricity in 1941.

Old church in Coopers Falls, the oldest building in town, May 2021 (D. Schneider-Gagné)

The Town's Decline

As the village's population increased with the arrival of new lumber workers, there was significant alcoholism due to the transient nature of many residents. Thomas Cooper was strongly opposed to alcohol and drunkenness, so he supported the temperance movement, banning the sale and consumption of alcohol. During their 50-year marriage, which resulted in nine children, Thomas traveled extensively to promote the temperance movement, leading him back to England and Scotland, where he lectured on the evils of alcohol.

While Coopers Falls was initially successful in its early years, the depletion of forest around town contributed to the decline in business, resulting in the closure of the lumber mill and local shops. Despite modern advancement and technology, which provided easier access and communication with Coopers Falls, the community slowly decreased until the last two buildings remaining, the general store and post office, were finally closed by Frank Cooper in in 1968.

Coopers Falls, as seen from the road, May 2021 (D. Schneider-Gagné)

The Remains of Coopers Falls

Today, Coopers Falls is a ghost town with an approximate population of ten to fourteen people. It's easy to spot on a drive or hike through the area, where you'll see the Methodist church, which is completely closed, and the occasional opening of St. George's Anglican Church, which hosts special services and events. When Thomas Cooper left town to travel and lecture to support the temperance movement, he left Coopers Falls to William, his son, who died tragically in 1921 due to a machine accident.

Throughout the mid-1900s and today, descendants of the Cooper family continue to reside in and around the town. Driving through the area, you'll notice a few dilapidated barns, sheds, and several buildings currently used for work and home. It's a scenic area that's ideal for hiking and exploring. However, "No Trespass" signs and fences along the ghost town's waterfalls indicate that it's privately owned, with heavily controlled access to most areas, including the Black River and surrounding properties.

An old shed in Coopers Falls, May 2021 (D. Schneider-Gagné)

Is Coopers Falls Haunted?

I noticed nothing peculiar while visiting the eerie but fascinating ghost town. The settlement's abandoned state creates a unique experience. I was drawn to explore as many spots within and around the town where there were no fences or obstructions. There appears to be a small auto shop and several houses where a handful of residents live. In my search for reports of the paranormal or unusual, I didn't find any reports or sightings in Coopers Falls. If the town is haunted by its past, Thomas Cooper may be the culprit, as its fervent supporter and enforcer of the temperance movement. Despite the lack of hauntings reported in the area, the untamed woods, lily-pad-covered ponds, and shadows of a once booming town are all worthwhile exploring during a drive, bike ride, or hike through the region.

Scenic view near the Severn River and bridge, en route to Coopers Falls from Washago, Ontario, May 2021 (D. Schneider-Gagné)

Hiking Through the Scenic Ghost Town

One of the best features in and around Coopers Falls is the eight-kilometer trail, with abundant natural beauty, from beaver ponds and deer and bird nesting areas to dense forests and wetlands. You'll find this hidden village of the past by driving north on Highway 400, where the road merges into Highway 11. Canal Road will take you over Severn Bridge and onto Coopers Falls Road, which leads into town. While many areas of the former town are privately owned, you'll still find many sites intact and beautiful scenery to enjoy during your visit.

6.

The Cabbagetown Monster (Toronto, Ontario)

Looking south on Parliament Street just north of Carlton in the Cabbagetown neighbourhood, Toronto, October 2021 (D. Schneider-Gagné)

One of Toronto's most popular urban legends is the Cabbagetown Monster. It was first reported in 1978 by a man who preferred to use only his first name, Ernest, when recounting his experience with the local newspaper. He lived between low-rise apartments and locally-owned shops in Cabbagetown, Toronto, a neighbourhood well-known for its Victorian-style homes and historic buildings. At this time, the city had an intricate underground tunnel system for sewage and waste, in addition to Toronto's subway tunnels and underground pathways in the downtown core.

The Story of Toronto's Most Infamous Urban Legend

Ernest initially discovered a small tunnel near his apartment on Parliament Street, a central road in the neighbourhood. He was either searching for a cat or simply curious about this narrow structure, so he investigated the opening using a flashlight. As he ventured further into the secret tunnel, he noticed movement just ahead of him, so he focused his eyes on what appeared to be a small animal.

As Ernest became aware of his surroundings, he felt a sinking sense of terror. It was not a household cat, dog, rodent, raccoon, or any other common urban animal. Instead, it resembled a monkey with a long tail, covered in grey fur, and about the size of a small child. The most unnerving feature was its green, glowing eyes, staring directly at Ernest - a frightening sight. According to Ernest's report, it hissed at him to say, "Go away!" Quickly, Ernest backed out of the small cavern, shaken by the experience but eager to share it with other city residents.

While no other sightings were reported, Ernest's story was published as an article in the local newspaper, and the urban legend became widespread and known as the Cabbagetown Monster. Other variations of this tale refer to the sighting as contact with an alien, or it is believed to be a mythical creature from ancient folklore. Ernest was considered to be a credible person, with no reason to fabricate this story, which later fueled many theories about Toronto's hidden waterway tunnels, including wild, sci-fi stories of secret aliens, an urban-dwelling bigfoot, or an undiscovered species of creatures living underground.

Many people have retold this tale over the years, which continues to fascinate new and long-time residents of the neighbourhood. While some people believe Ernest mistook a large rodent or raccoon for a monster, the unusual tale has become an intriguing part of the city's collection of urban legends.

References in Literature and Film

One of the most well-known references to the Cabbagetown Monster in modern film is a 2008 movie, Toronto Stories, which premiered at the Toronto International Film Festival. The movie is a collection of four tales about individual people's lives and how they interact with each other in unexpected ways. One of the tales follows a children's quest for an underground monster, in the Cabbagetown neighbourhood, alongside the search for a missing child.

Unsolved Mystery or an Urban Animal Sighting?

While many people dismissed the reporting of the Cabbagetown Monster as nothing more than an exaggeration of an urban animal sighting, many tales surfaced about strange and unusual ongoings beneath the city's surface. Some people imagined a secret alien operation, a city-dwelling bigfoot, or a human-like creature that lived in a hidden underground tunnel system. References to ancient cultures and stories of indigenous legends have also been mentioned, though the most likely culprit, according to most, is an over-sized urban animal, who frightened a local man. His perception of the experience may have been amplified by the dim lighting and elongated shadows of the narrow tunnel.

7.

Preston Springs Hotel (Cambridge, Ontario)

The front view of the Preston Springs Hotel from the corner of King and Fountain Street in Cambridge (Preston), Ontario, July 2020 (D. Schneider-Gagné)

The Preston Springs Hotel was an iconic landmark that I first noticed during long bicycle rides in the early 1990s throughout the Waterloo region, where I grew up. It's a magnificent structure that captures your attention from any direction, whether driving north from Galt or east from Hespeler towards Preston or gliding on your bike from the south end of Kitchener. In 2020, the abandoned hotel was scheduled for demolition, which had become a divisive issue, with local historians and admirers proposing to declare it a heritage building; however, the hotel's structure was deemed unsafe and irreparable for future use or access. In early January 2021, the building was finally taken down.

The History of the Preston Springs Hotel

A distant view of the old Preston Springs Hotel, July 2020 (D. Schneider-Gagné)

The Preston Springs Hotel was built in the 1870s and officially opened in 1888 as one of the area's most luxurious retreats. It included a spa, a retirement residence, and naval training barracks. It was located at the corner of King Street and Fountain Street in Preston, a town that later amalgamated with Hespeler and Galt to form the city of Cambridge.

Originally, the resort was named Del Monte Hotel, inspired by the hotel's architectural design of the same name in Monterey, California. The retreat quickly became a well-known tourist destination, offering a stunning visual of the Preston landscape. The hotel's convenient location, towards the north end of Preston, made it relatively easy to find, especially for visitors traveling through this part of the town. Near the turn of the century, the hotel was extended to twice its size towards Fountain Street, where it became prominently visible.

By the 1920s, it was renamed the Preston Springs Hotel due to its natural mineral springs, terrace gardens, and orchards, a stunning interior with a fireplace, a wide staircase to three levels, and outdoor access to five acres of natural beauty. It became a popular destination for celebrities, politicians, and notable individuals, including Lord Stanley, the famous UK politician famous for the Stanley Cup, and Lucy Maud Montgomery, the author of Anne of Green Gables.

Throughout the 1920s, two doctors from Toronto, Gordon Hagmeier and J. Edwin, along with the change of the hotel's name, transformed the building into a private clinic and sanitarium. In 1943, A.R. Kaufman, a notable philanthropist from Kitchener, bought the building and then handed it to the federal government so that it could be used to provide housing for trainees for the Women's Royal Canadian Naval Training Establishment, located in nearby Galt.

Since then, the once-famous luxury hotel has become a long-term retirement care facility. In the 1970s, Alan Hodge bought the building. Despite his efforts to redevelop and renovate the structure, it eventually fell into disrepair due to neglect, causing the interior of the old hotel to become dangerous. It was finally closed in 1990. The city of Cambridge's chief building official eventually issued an order to demolish the site, which took place in January 2021 after several years of consideration, debate, and postponement.

The secured exterior of the former Preston Springs Hotel, July 2020 (D. Schneider-Gagné)

Our Visit to the Preston Springs Hotel Site in July 2020

We took a day trip to Cambridge to view the old hotel site, which appeared eerily similar to how I remembered it in the early 1990s, shortly after it was permanently closed. Immediately, we noticed that all the doors and windows, including any potential opening, were secured with boards. There was a lot of graffiti towards the rear of the building, where the ground was sloped, and completed fenced off. Any slight possibility of finding a way inside was minimal and unsafe, so we didn't attempt it.

Paranormal Sightings and Ghost Stories

A close-up view of the boarded-up hotel, July 2020 (D. Schneider-Gagné)

Over the years, many reports of paranormal activity throughout the hotel have occurred. Curious urban explorers encountered the interior, gutted rooms, empty elevator shafts, shards of raw materials, discarded shower curtains, and unsettling stillness. It's as if the building was frozen in time, in the year 1990. While the building was in its last days as a retirement home, residents were neglected, and the long-term home went into receivership. Due to funding and staffing shortages, retirees sometimes lacked adequate food or care.

There are reports that Alan Hodge, who tried to keep the structure intact, made efforts to dissuade vandalism and destruction of the property to no avail. In one story, he entered the defunct building after noticing a light on the fourth floor and investigating further as he climbed the stairs. As he reached the top, he was violently pushed down the stairs. When he quickly looked up towards where he fell, there was a mysterious human-like figure with a frightening smile and a transparent torso.

Many visitors to the site reported feeling uneasy, cold, and uncomfortable. It was believed that some of the previous residents haunted the building and expressed anger due to abuse and neglect. In the final years nearing the building's demolition, boards and fencing prevented curious explorers from investigating the old hotel. Anyone able to find a small space or opening inside would find lots of dust, debris, and, at times, difficulty navigating through the building due to little or no lighting. Some brave visitors who dared to sneak through the vacant remains would report a feeling that they weren't alone, as if a mysterious entity was carefully observing their curious exploration.

Light switches moving, wiring suddenly loosening and falling from a secure place, and other odd experiences were often noticed. In one incident, an electrical wire, thought to be stationary, unexpectedly swung down, nearly hitting someone in the face. In other reports, items would suddenly appear where they hadn't been without any logical explanation. This led some people to believe they were intentionally moved by a prankster or poltergeist activity. The abandoned elevator shaft, an eerie sight on its own, was often described as ice cold, even when the remainder of the building was moderate or warm in temperature.

Some hallways, slanted and uneven, angling upward, lead to the empty elevator shaft. The temperature in this area would become so cold that your breath was visible. While the basement was cooler than the rest of the building, it was not nearly as chilled as these hallways. During those years, as the building stood vacant and still, many believed that the spirit of the former owner, Alan Hodge, currently resided on the fourth floor, keeping watch over anyone who dared to enter. While the now-demolished site has yet to be developed, many wonder how the former hotel's vibrant history and darker presence may continue to haunt the area.

8.

The Mackenzie House (Toronto, Ontario)

The Mackenzie House on Bond Street in Toronto, September 2023 (D. Schneider-Gagné)

If you were to pass by the Mackenzie House on Bond Street, just east of Yonge Street, in the downtown core, you would most likely miss it unless you were searching for this unique, historic building. The three-story house, extended to accommodate staff, a gift shop, and tours, is set in from the road, offering a plain, Georgian-style design without any distinguishing features. Today, it's considered a heritage attraction in the city and one of Toronto's most haunted places.

The History of the Mackenzie House

The restored building was originally built in or around the 1850s, providing a home to several individuals and families, most notably a former mayor and leader of the Rebellion, William Lyon Mackenzie. It's a fascinating site that features an old printing press from the mid-1840s, currently situated in the basement, which Mackenize famously used to print his newsletter. His publications often contained articles about his political views, considered radical and controversial at the time. The house is well known as the mayor's home, despite only having lived in the residence, along with this family, for about two years, between 1859 and 1861.

Tours are regularly offered in the house, and there are education programs for children and adults. During a historical tour of the home, you'll find each of the original rooms, including the living room, dining area, kitchen, and bedrooms, completely preserved with nineteenth-century furniture, fixtures, paintings, artwork, and clothing. The site is often featured in city-sponsored events, including art festivals and installations. It's also a popular spot to explore during ghost tours.

Who's Haunting the Mackenzie House?

There are numerous reports of hauntings in the historic abode, ranging from sudden changes in lighting to full apparitions and poltergeist activity. It's one of two buildings in the City of Toronto where the history of hauntings is recorded, in writing, on a government plaque or document; the other property is the Gibraltar Lighthouse, located on the Toronto Islands. While many of the early reports of hauntings were debunked or considered unsubstantiated, further disturbances and consistent reports from different people, including visitors and site staff, prompted several investigations into the activity.

The window in the upper right corner of the Mackenzie House, the bedroom of William Lyon Mackenzie - do you see a face in the window? August, 2013 (Colleen J. Cairney)

The most common sightings in the Mackenzie house are the previous mayor, who can be seen wandering from one room to the next, wearing a wig and an old housecoat. Sometimes, a woman is seen in the house with a white gown and long, dark brown hair. When early reports were made in the mid-1950s and 1960s, an exorcism was performed by John Frank, an Anglican Archdeacon, with a reporter present, Aubrey Wice from the Telegram. Shortly after that, the private ownership of the home was transferred to a non-profit organization, and the city now preserves it as a historic site.

Apparitions of various kinds are among the most common sightings in the Mackenzie House. The former home residents, the Mackenzie family, are often seen on the second and third floors, where preserved rooms are kept as close as possible to their original state. Due to the conditions in the nineteenth century, William and his wife, Elizabeth, had thirteen children, of which only six survived to adulthood. The mayor also passed away in his bed, ending the two years of occupancy in the home. It is often believed that Mackenzie is most commonly reported in and around the main bedroom due to living his last days within that space, and leaving behind the energy that lingers in the house.

Inside the Mackenzie house. Several orbs appear in the photo, August, 2013 (Colleen J. Cairney)

Poltergeist activity is the movement of objects, by spirits, ghosts, or some unexplainable phenomenon, from one spot to another. These paranormal sightings can be quiet, and barely noticeable at first, later escalating to violent throwing or hurling of items, slamming doors, and other aggressive sounds throughout the house. Staff have reported feeling like they're being watched when no one is physically in a room. They also hear the piano playing on the main floor, only to find no one present, and the music suddenly stops when they enter the room. The turning on and off of faucets, flickering lights, cold spots, and a heavy, eerie sensation are frequently reported, in varying degrees, by visitors to the home.

The printing press is another source of paranormal activity. Several staff members have reported hearing the sounds of the press moving, as if running off copies of a newsletter, only to find the machine completely stopped and instantly quiet upon investigating. Due to the numerous reports of unexplainable activity in the house, a reporter accompanied and recorded Anglican Archdeacon John Frank performing an exorcism as he entered each room throughout the historic residence.

Following this event, the house became the property of the City of Toronto in 1960, and it is currently a museum and a historical site. This transfer of ownership is often jokingly mentioned to include all the contents of the house and one exorcised ghost. The Mackenzie House has received its share of visitors from the media, intrigued fans of the supernatural, and paranormal investigators.

Our Experiences in the Mackenzie House

After one ghost tour near the Halloween season over ten years ago, I was immediately impressed by the haunted history of the Mackenzie House and tales of unusual activity occurring over decades. When my children were young, they occasionally enjoyed visiting the historic site, as there were (and still are) family-themed activities. When they expressed a keen interest in joining a ghost tour, we booked one around Halloween and have since returned a handful of times to explore the home and see if we could pick up on any unusual sensations or activity.

While I didn't notice any cold spots throughout the house, I did feel a certain heaviness in the main bedroom, which is notorious as the former mayor's last place of rest before his death. The flickering of the electrified gas lighting and the eerie dancing of shadows across the room's interior walls produced a spooky effect, which was slightly dizzying. The sensation didn't last long and quickly subsided as I left the room and returned downstairs with the rest of the ghost tour group.

Several photos taken by a friend and me show orbs and other irregular lighting that may be due to dust particles, camera settings, or unexplained phenomena. One photo, taken by my friend, just outside the house, appears to reveal a man's face from the top right window, between the square-shaped window frames, which is the famous bedroom of William Lyon Mackenzie. Orbs and unusual lighting tend to plague many pictures taken inside the house, though one plausible explanation could be the dust from preserved objects and furniture. I found that having a heightened awareness of the reported activity in this home, gave me an increased state of expectation, where every creak in the flooring, on the stairs, or flicker of a flame can set off a quick jump scare.

Is the Paranormal Activity Real or Imaginary?

Are the hauntings of the Mackenzie House real, an exaggeration, or completely fabricated? Many reports of hauntings and unusual activities crept up later in the home's existence, starting in the mid-twentieth century, with some residents having no experiences of any kind and others noticing lots of phenomena. Since no one resides in the house currently, it is managed by staff, who experience the most recent hauntings. The most commonly reported sightings include the phantom running of the printing press in the basement, footsteps upstairs without anyone present, and objects being moved periodically throughout the house. Most people enjoy the Mackenzie House's haunted history as an intriguing part of the city's urban history.

9.

Hermitage Ruins (Hamilton, Ontario)

The estate remains of the Hermitage Ruins, during a hike through the Conservation area in July 2020 (D. Schneider-Gagné)

The Hermitage Ruins, also known as the "Hermitage," are the remains of an estate and property bought in 1855 by George Gordon Browne Leith, where he lived with his wife and children. Before acquiring this land, Reverend Sheed bought it in 1830, where a house frame was built, and apples were stored in the surrounding orchard until 1900. Reverend Sheed, a Presbyterian minister in Ancaster, was considered the home's first resident until he died in 1832.

The History of the Hermitage Ruins

Before Leith purchased the property, the area was bought and sold several times. One of the most notable past residents, Otto Ives, arrived in Canada from England. His wife, who was originally from Greece, accompanied him. As they settled into their newly purchased home in 1833 with their immediate and extended family, they hired staff, including a coachman, who played a pivotal role in the site's reported paranormal sightings.

The estate, built by George Gordon Brown Leith, remained with his family for many years. In the 1860s, the estate included 150 acres of well-developed farmland and a stone house to accommodate a family of eight and five staff members. They remained on the site until the death of Leith in 1887, followed by his wife in 1900. Their daughter, Alma Dick-Lauder, took over the property in later years, residing on the estate until 1942. A fire in 1934 destroyed the buildings, and over time, the property returned to the original forest it was nearly a century earlier. Today, the property is rich in large trees, vines, plants, wildlife, and waterfalls.

The Hamilton Conservation Authority bought the property, including 120 acres of land in the Dundas Valley, from Charles Hill, the owner at the time. While this historic property became known as the Hermitage, the original stone house and nearby structures now exist in ruins and have become a popular destination for outdoor explorers, weddings, local concerts, and ghost tours.

The forested area around the Hermitage Ruins, July 2020 (D. Schneider-Gagné)

A Tragic Tale of Love and Loss

Smaller ruins surrounding the site of the former estate, July 2020 (D. Schneider-Gagné)

During Otto Ives' residence at the Hermitage, his coachman, William Black, fell in love with his wife's niece, who had followed the family to Canada and settled into the estate. William conjured enough courage to ask Mr. Ives' permission to marry, and when he did, his request was immediately refused. He was devastated, as during this era, it was custom and expected that permission from the future bride's father was necessary, or no wedding would result.

The following day, after William Black absorbed the devastating news, Otto and his family did not see him appear with the carriage, as routinely expected. When a search ensued, he was discovered hanging from the rafters of the stable, where he died by suicide. Since William died in this manner, he could not be buried in the village's churchyard and, instead, was laid to rest in an area where Sulphur Springs Road and Lover's Lane cross.

Reported Hauntings at the Hermitage Ruins

Close-up of the well-preserved ruins, July 2020 (D. Schneider-Gagné)

According to some visitors, the tragic cries of the coachman echo through the forest, especially during the evening or night. The sight of overgrown vegetation and abandoned ruins offers a unique, ominous experience, which only appears more creepy and foreboding after dark. While the Hermitage Ruins are popular for many events, they are locally famous for ghost walks, curious explorers, and paranormal investigators.

The heartbroken coachman is the center of an urban legend. The legend states that if you visit the Hermitage ruins on a full moon, you'll see William Black walking between the ruins and the carriage house, calling for his love. Some reports include sightings of the heartbroken coachman around Lover's Lane, where his body was buried. He appears to wander, looking for his love, only to be trapped in a realm of sorrow and loss.

According to some guests, visuals of glowing corpses emerge around the ruins, only to sink into the ground. A woman, often believed to be the coachman's lost love, is seen wandering on what used to be the second floor of the building. The coachman and his love are also seen walking together, arms linked, through the nearby forest, only to disappear. One of the most spectacular sightings reported is the entire mansion, appearing in its former state, in full structural details, with candlelight, as if completely restored, only to disappear into the night. Imagine seeing an 1800s estate suddenly materialize, as if traveling back in time, only to vaporize into the dark!

Ghost sightings and local urban legends of the Hermitage ruins continue to bring many people to the site. Due to the high volume of reports, including one of the founding partners of local groups and investigators, many people are drawn to this location, hoping to experience sightings of silhouettes against the ruins and other phenomena. Regular ghost walks are conducted at night, when the most eerie, unusual experiences are likely to occur. During the day, the site is accessible through the conservation area for hiking and exploring nature.

Railway tracks and old station located in the conservation area, July 2020 (D. Schneider-Gagné)

Our Visit to the Hermitage Ruins

In July 2020, we hiked through the conservation area, which is located in Ancaster, adjacent to the city of Hamilton. It's a short distance from downtown Hamilton and an ideal place to explore if you're a nature enthusiast or interested in historic sites. Our trek through the woods took us through lush greenery, tall trees, rich plant life, a closed train station, and train tracks. Once we reached the ruins, we found them well-preserved but uneventful. After taking photos of the remaining exterior walls, we continued hiking the conservation area without unusual or unexplainable experiences.

While we didn't encounter any paranormal activity, most of the reports from other visitors indicated a higher level of activity during the evening or night. Ghost walks and related tours are sometimes offered at the ruins, usually moreso in the summer and fall, and they've become a popular spot for anyone intrigued with the local history and lore, including paranormal researchers. It's also a popular spot for weddings and photography for various occasions.

10.
The Beck House (Penetanguishene, Ontario)

Photo of the Beck mansion in Penetanguishine, Ontario, in August 2022 (D. Schneider-Gagné)

At first glance, the Queen Anne Revival-style structure is an impressive sight. Like many notorious buildings with a dark past, the Beck Mansion is considered one of the most haunted places in Ontario. It's a historic, restored home that houses long-term residents, and one apartment on the top floor is available as a short-term rental for overnight, weekend, and longer stays. It's a unique lodging that attracts fans of historical sites, paranormal investigators, and enthusiasts.

Penetanguishene is well known for its hauntings and reports of the supernatural. These notable structures include the Centennial Museum, which used to be the town's general store, and the Beck Mansion, which is often considered one of the top destinations for paranormal investigators in Ontario, Canada. It's one of those rare places where you're most likely to experience something unusual, whether you're a skeptic or a firm believer in the supernatural.

The Beck Mansion's History and Legacy

In 1885, Carl Beck built the iconic house, which offers a unique design unlike any homes in Penetanguishene. One of the mansion's distinguishing features is the slate roof, the only house with this style in town. He was well known as one of the wealthiest men in the region and one of the most successful lumber magnates. Between 1892 and 1895, Carl Beck was mayor of the town and established his presence with a family of nine children by purchasing the first automobile available in the area, which was a 1903 Oldsmobile.

While the Beck family lived in relative luxury at their Victorian residence, Beck's wife tragically passed away, which led Mary, the eldest, to care for the children. She raised her siblings as the primary caregiver for years, assuming a maternal position, which would have been an exhausting, difficult role to fulfill. Upon Carl Beck's death, each of his children would receive a fair portion of his estate, except Mary, who only received one dollar. This unjust inheritance is believed to have caused Mary's spirit to linger and haunt the mansion.

The Hauntings of Beck Mansion

Reports of hauntings at the Beck House vary from doors opening on their own and the lingering scent of cigar smoke to full apparitions, disembodied voices, and moving objects. It's a popular spot for paranormal investigations and anyone wishing to catch a glimpse of Mary or several spirits or entities believed to have never left. Imagine getting ready to fall asleep in one of the bedroom's cozy king-size beds, only to have a pair of invisible hands tuck you in, placing the blankets around you as you lie down. A sudden knock on the door or window, followed by an indistinguishable whisper or voice where no one is present, would likely keep you from enjoying a good night's rest.

Based on the sheer number of reports on unexplainable activities in the Beck Mansion, it's common for many visitors to relate at least one or two unusual experiences during their stay in the top-floor apartment. Strange noises, finding an object moved to another spot, and flickering lights are among the most common reports. Mary is often considered the culprit of the hauntings, whether her silhouette graces the windows from the outside or makes her presence known within the home.

In some discussions about the Beck House, paranormal investigators estimate there are close to twenty spirits, ghosts, or energies in the house. One or more of them are actively haunting the mansion at any time. While this claim isn't substantiated and would be difficult to prove, most people who have experienced unexplained events in the house believe more than one entity is responsible for the hauntings.

The interior staircase of the Beck House, August 2022 (D. Schneider-Gagné)

Our Unforgettable Visit to the Beck House

As soon as I learned of the infamous Beck Mansion and its legacy of the supernatural, I was determined to book an overnight stay. I visited with the youngest of my three kids and a friend, making the trek from Toronto to Penetranguishene for two days in late August 2022. Once we settled into the apartment, we noticed one of the bedroom doors, which was decorated in red, would open on its own. While this wasn't too unexpected at first, we ensured the windows were closed and the fans turned off, isolating any causes or drafts inside the room. Despite our efforts, the door continued to open, sometimes a bit slower, then slightly quicker, and at unexpected times. We observed this door throughout our stay, as we stood still, and remained silent to not disturb or impact any factors that may contribute to its movement.

There was an uncanny feeling that we weren't alone, whether in the apartment or just outside the unit in the house's lobby. We also felt this sensation while outside on the front lawn of the property. While we didn't notice any unusual scents or the movement of objects, there was the quiet but distinct sound of someone talking towards the evening. It was slight, like a conversation on the television in another room, but everything was turned off for the night. It could have been easily dismissed as a peripheral sound from a neighboring unit or a conversation outside, only we were situated on the top floor, and all the windows were closed.

Around three o'clock in the morning, we decided to have fun with a smartphone app that took EVP recordings. EVP or electronic voice projection recordings are traditionally done with a digital or analogue recorder by paranormal researchers. The device must be placed in an area of the room or space without interference, such as a window or vent that may cause noise. It is believed to pick up and magnify undetectable sounds and disturbances from another realm, such as a knock, faint music, or even a trace of a voice, often attributed to spirits or phenomena.

We chose the red-themed bedroom as the best spot for our little experiment due to the mysterious opening door, which continued to open at varying speeds throughout the night. I didn't intentionally close it to see what would happen if we left it open. During the recordings, there were no distinct sounds in real-time, nor were there any sightings or movements within our immediate space. It wasn't until later when we played back the recordings, that we heard what sounded like a woman breathing and a clear "knock" when we asked if any entities wanted to communicate with us. We asked, "If you want to communicate with us, tap once for yes and two for no." In response, we heard what sounded like one tap or knock. Initially, it wasn't very distinguishable from the background.

We made several recordings, with two of us using different smartphone apps to capture "evidence" of anything entering the house. When we played back one of the recordings, we could hear a distinct heartbeat towards the end, which lasted for about four to five seconds. We replayed this section several times to ensure we heard it correctly. This was preceded by someone moving around the phone and breathing lightly, in the recording. We positioned our phones on a vanity table during each recording where no interference or obstruction would cause unwanted noise. The results of the recordings intrigued us and made for great conversation when we returned home from our excursion!

If you decide to visit the Beck Mansion, you'll find it's often booked up in advance, due to its popularity. It's a unique place to spend one or two nights, whether you're an enthusiast of the paranormal or a skeptic or simply enjoy Victorian architecture. There is a journal that contains personal writings and experiences by numerous visitors to the mansion. The hosts are very welcoming, and it's a relaxing spot to spend the weekend. It's a unique part of the town's interesting history, and a great tourist attraction.

11.

Newmarket Ghost Canal (Newmarket, Ontario)

A view of the canal under a bridge in Newmarket, Ontario, September 2023 (D. Schneider-Gagné)

Canal systems were one of the most pivotal ways to travel throughout Southern Ontario. In the mid to late 1800s, canals were ideal for transportation throughout many regions in the province before the expansion of the railway system, which provided an efficient alternative, rendering the canal system unnecessary. Today, the Newmarket ghost canal follows a scenic nature trail along the Holland River in Newmarket, Ontario.

The History of the Newmarket Ghost Canal

Despite political debate over the canal's construction and the lack of need for the Trent Severn Canal due to nearby railway access, the project commenced in 1908. While some people favoured the idea of its construction, several surveys indicated it would not be sustainable, and there wouldn't be sufficient water to fill the canal for its intended purpose. As the canal system was developed, railway tracks extended to cover many new towns and settlements while regularly delivering products, raw materials, and people.

Additional problems impacted the usefulness of the canal. Due to the low amount of water flowing into the Holland River, the supply would be limited to fill the canal for at least one season. Railway access, which ran close to the river and canal system, became a steady reminder of how inefficient the dead-end canal would be and the lack of support local businesses and people would receive from this project.

The construction continued despite these concerns, and a well-established train system in the area has existed since the mid-1800s. Since the project was led by a prominent political figure, Wilfrid Laurier, with the support of local government and media, financial support poured into the canal's construction. Silas Seymour, a chief engineer on the project in 1883, said, "Canals, as a successful and necessary means of transport, have outlived their usefulness."

The Abandoned Canal: A Scenic Nature Trail Today

While the original intent of the Newmarket ghost canal was unsustainable, the sixteen-kilometer route provides a scenic trail for cycling, hiking, and canoeing. It's a beautiful passage meant to connect the Trent Severn Waterway with Lake Simcoe and East Holland River. When I visited the hiking trail, I could easily access the various canal locks along the path, though some areas are fenced off and difficult to access due to safety concerns. During rainy weather, the forested areas surrounding the trails and canal are slippery, increasing the risk of falling and injury.

Depending on your pace, the trail takes one hour and a half to hike. There is plenty of incredible wildlife and rich nature, so I paused often, extending my hike to nearly two hours. When I reached the second lock of the canal, I noticed a small opening below the bridge, giving me narrow access. I carefully navigated to a few spots below, where I could catch a broader view of the canal's remnants. There are layers of colorful graffiti, partially finished stairways, and worn infrastructure of what could have been a fascinating waterway across the region for boaters.

Today, the Nokiidaa Trail, alongside the abandoned canals, is ideal for picturesque nature walks, wildlife spotting, birdwatching, and photography. Over one hundred years later, it's an excellent place to visit year-round on a bike or foot. The ghost canal features a reservoir, a filled-in basin, several locks, a swing bridge, and wonderful views from all angles of each site.

Lock two of the abandoned ghost canal system along the Holland River in Newmarket, Ontario, September 2023 (D. Schneider-Gagné)

Is the Ghost Canal Haunted?

When I visited the ghost canal, I'll admit that the eerie remains, worn structures, and fenced-off access felt unwelcoming initially. However, I quickly grew curious about the canal and surrounding area, which became more intriguing during my hike. While the history of the canal system is riddled with political debate and unsound financial decisions, it represents an integral part of Newmarket's development. As I researched this site, I didn't find any urban legends, spooky tales, or paranormal reports of any kind. Since the project wasn't fully completed, little or nothing is known about the workers or the condition of the work environment during its construction.

Newmarket is an interesting city with numerous modern and historical structures, ghost tales, and hauntings to explore, including the city's town hall. It's a great spot to explore paranormal stories and sites, whether you join a ghost walk or investigate independently. The ghost canal is also a unique place that offers fantastic scenery, and a glimpse into the town's development history.

<h1 style="text-align:center">12.</h1>

The Malabar Costume Shop (Toronto, Ontario)

The Malabar costume shop, permanently closed, on McCaul Street in downtown Toronto, June 2023 (D. Schneider-Gagné)

One of the most iconic costume stores in downtown Toronto, Malabar, was well known for featuring a variety of unique, high-quality dancewear, costumes, make-up, theatrical props, and accessories. Its most recent location, on 14 McCaul Street, just a short distance from OCAD University (Ontario College of Art and Design), has since closed in March 2022. However, its legacy remains as a once memorable place to visit. Its final location was in a historical building known for its professional staff, one-of-a-kind items, and stories of a haunted freight elevator.

The History of the Malabar

Initially, the costume shop began in Winnipeg, Manitoba, as a family business in 1923. Sara Mallabar originally opened the shop, and later, a Toronto location was opened by her son, Harry Mallabar. While the store was initially spelled "Mallabar" after the founder, it was later changed to a single "L" and soon set up shop in downtown Toronto with a storefront on Spadina Street. Then, in 1932, the business relocated to King Street West for just over two decades. After a devastating fire at this site, Malabar Ltd. moved to its final location in 1957, on McCaul Street. The shop was well known for its impressive selection of high-quality theatrical costumes, often bought or rented for galas, operas, musicals, and other events.

The Malabar offered rental services to companies throughout North America, with the help of a large inventory of items located at the retail shop and in a separate warehouse, which housed an incredible 30,000 costumes. The store's staff were make-up, theatre, special effects, props, and costume design experts. They often collaborated with artists to create unique performance wear and costumes for various events, including Halloween and themed parties. Despite the store's overwhelming success, the business eventually closed its doors in early 2022. As of mid-2023, the building remains vacant, offering a historic glimpse into the past.

A Brief Visit to the Infamous Malabar

I regret that I didn't spend much time getting familiar with the Malabar, though I was impressed with the store's vibrant displays, friendly staff, and unique selection of costumes, wigs, and props. On more than one occasion, I passed by the storefront after hours while enjoying the city's entertaining downtown core and at least once on a ghost tour, where I learned about interesting reports of paranormal sightings and bizarre, unexplained experiences involving the shop's freight elevator.

Costume Shop Hauntings

Imagine you're working late at night at the Malabar, checking the displays, closing the cash register, and saying goodbye to co-workers as they leave before you close the store. No one is left, so you're entirely alone. It's a quiet, calming experience because you're accustomed to the place but notice a sudden movement. A dash of white flashes then disappears behind a display rack. Is it the store's lighting? Then, it happens again; only this time, you see what appears to be the figure of a woman dressed in white, making a startling presence, only to fade again into one of the displays or corners of the costume shop. Many employees of the Malabar reported sightings of the lady in white or a similar presence, usually seen in and around the clothing and costume displays, especially in the storage area.

Another presence in the store was often believed to be the ghost of Sara Malabar, the shop's original owner. Some have claimed to feel her spirit near the photocopier. A few staff members claim Mrs. Malabar is kind and helpful because when they mention her in the shop or ask for help, a jammed stack of paper or photocopy printout that doesn't turn out will improve soon thereafter.

The most infamous ghostly presence in the costume shop is the elevator man, who was tragically killed while repairing the manual lift in the historic building in the 1960s. The incident involved a snapped cable, which sent the elevator car crashing to the bottom floor, resulting in the technician's death from the impact. While there were no reports of poltergeist activity, employees often felt fearful or at least apprehensive of using the elevator, preferring to take the stairs. Numerous reports and tales of a haunting presence in the historic shop have surfaced over the years in magazine articles, in blogs, and posted on forums.

13.

Albion Falls (Hamilton, Ontario)

View of the Albion Falls, in Hamilton, Ontario, September 2022 (D. Schneider-Gagné)

Hamilton, Ontario is considered the waterfall capital of the world, with over 150 waterfalls within the city's limits. Albion Falls is one of the most popular sites in King's Forest at Red Hill Creek, which is nestled in Hamilton's east end. The water cascades down layers of rocks, smoothly worn, descending and widening towards the creek, which is part of the Niagara Escarpment. It's easily visible from one or two observation platforms, which can be reached from a hiking trail. The higher viewing deck is open, while the lower platform is closed. Rocks in the area were added to two of the city's most famous attractions, the

Royal Botanical Gardens and Hamilton's Rock Garden. It's a beautiful place to visit year-round, especially during the warmer seasons.

The History of Albion Falls

Albion Falls is located in an area that was once the Village of Mount Albion. Due to its potential for water supply, the property around the falls was granted to William Davis just before 1792, when he left North Carolina for Canada. The 500 acres surrounding Albion Falls were developed into a settlement to include blacksmith shops, a church, a grist mill, a general store, and several taverns. The main road through this town, which was later established as Albion Mills in 1880, was named Mud Street and is still called this today.

By the late 1800s, the city of Hamilton was incorporated, and a toll road charged a fee for each return trip by horse-drawn wagon. Up until just after the turn of the twentieth century, the mill continued to operate, and Mount Albion offered a few interesting features: it contained a strong sulphur spring that frothed up from a shallow, drilled hole. The water was strong, it didn't freeze too quickly, and worked consistently well on farmland, which was ideal for local agriculture. During the mid-1800s, a dam and a sawmill were located in a nearby valley, where two streams and waterfalls convene: Mill Falls and Buttermilk Falls.

A Dark Past and Hauntings of Albion Falls

For over a century, the Albion Falls and surrounding land became notorious for several tragic events and reports of paranormal sightings. At the turn of the century, Robert Grassie, the owner of the mill, fell into the wheel pit and was killed. Due to the accident, the mill was shut down permanently in 1907. In the mid-1800s, an argument between two workers resulted in one of them getting killed at the sawmill, and later, visitors to the area claimed to see his ghost hovering over the water in the stream. In other reports, passersby would see him wandering through the woods or along the local roads by the falls.

The dense forest around Mount Albion was, and still is, considered haunted, where spirits lurk at night. One visitor to the Black Horse Tavern in Mount Albion claimed to see a spirit or ghost near a tree one night. When he attempted to swing at the figure with his fist, he realized it was the hanging corpse of a freshly slaughtered pig. While this encounter was likely clouded by intoxication, other people claim to have experienced supernatural phenomena around Albion Falls.

When Jane Reilly's heart was broken after the love of her life, Joseph Rousseau, abandoned her; she fell to her death over the waterfall. Joseph's mother, Mrs. Rousseau, had encouraged her son to break off the relationship, though just before her death, she claimed to feel Jane's hand touch her shoulders when she visited the site. Other bodies discovered at Albion Falls include Evelyn Dick, an accused murderer, and an infamous bootlegger, Rocco Perri. Hamilton was also well known for the city's close connection to organized crime and related crimes throughout the 1900s.

During the 1950s, Albion Falls became one of the top spots for young visitors on foot or bicycle. It was popular for its natural beauty, quiet ambiance, and a local, small general store offering a drink and snack for the hike. Once the store was closed in 1960, the area remained popular for treks to view the waterfall, where some people took the risk of walking across the ledge and the lower areas of the creek towards the bottom of the falls.

A Scenic Visit to the Albion Falls

I visited the Albion Falls in September 2022. It's accessible by car through the exit on Dartnell Road, off the Lincoln Alexander Parkway. From the left lane, a left turn will bring you to Stonechurch Road East, where several large stores are located. You'll find Mud Street just a short distance from Pritchard Road. A similar route is easy to follow on bicycle, on foot, or with the city's public transit.

There are two platforms where the falls can be viewed, though the more distant observation deck was the only option I could access during my visit. It's scenic, where you'll find beautiful areas to hike and explore. A parking lot and paved walking path make it easy for pedestrians and cyclists to visit.

14.

Bowmanville POW Camp (Bowmanville, Ontario)

POW Camp, also known as Camp 30, on the outskirts of Bowmanville, Ontario, May 2022 (D. Schneider-Gagné)

When you hike to the outskirts of Bowmanville, Ontario, you'll discover a series of dilapidated ruins. It's a unique view into the site's past, when a series of buildings were constructed for a reformatory school in 1925. Over the past century, this area was nearly demolished, though it remains protected, to some extent as a heritage site, due to its historic significance.

The History of Camp 30

While the buildings were originally intended for a reformatory school in Bowmanville, the site was soon transformed during WWII, when it became a POW (prisoner of war) camp, where German soldiers were captured and detained during this time. Among the prisoners were Wolfgang Heyda and Otto Kretschmer, U-boat commanders who were well-known at the time. The site is often referred to as Camp 30, and it is the last standing and intact POW camp in Canada today.

The site was fairly modern in comparison to other POW camps across Canada, and today, it is the only fully intact site of all forty POW camps during WWII. Its unique characteristics included a theatre, a concert stage, and an indoor swimming pool, which were unlikely at other POW sites. Despite these luxuries, a barbed wire surrounding the fenced-in prison reminded them of their capture and inability to leave. There was only one escape attempt recorded among the forty POW sites across Canada in 1941, though there were likely more that hadn't been noted at the time. This event was later referred to as the "Battle of Bowmanville," involving an uprising by the German POWs, which resulted in the Canadian Armed Forces being called in to put an end to the developing chaos.

Due to the campus-style layout of this property, a number of private schools utilized the buildings and outdoor space easily, which included a generating plant, sports fields, and other projects. The final school located at the site, the Darul Uloom Islamic University, left in 2008, and within a year, the site was purchased privately by the Kaitlin Group for development.

One of the remaining historic Camp 30 buildings, May 2022 (D. Schneider-Gagné)

Bowmanville's Camp 30 Future

Many residents consider Camp 30 a historical site and worthy of protection from demolition and development. This advice was forwarded to the municipality of Clarington by Ontario Heritage. As a result, six of the original 18 structures were deemed a heritage site, which the Register of Properties of Cultural Heritage Value or Interest protects. Despite this effort to maintain these original buildings, which include the POW camp site, they have endured a lot of vandalism, at least one fire, and substantial erosion over time due to a lack of maintenance. The surrounding unprotected buildings, not included in the six designated as having heritage significance, are located north and south of this area and may be demolished to make room for a new housing development.

Discussions between the municipality and the Kaitlin Group resulted in the agreement to demolish only up to eight buildings, specifically those with the least historic or architectural value, so they can be repurposed or rebuilt as storage or locker rooms. The structures that held the most historical significance included the infirmary, dormitories, and concert hall. These structures remain on the site today, at 2020 Lambs Road in Bowmanville, which attracts locals, curious visitors, and urban explorers.

A peek inside of the remaining Camp 30 buildings, May 2022 (D. Schneider-Gagné)

Interior of one of the remaining Camp 30 buildings, May 2022 (D. Schneider-Gagné)

The Restoration Debate

As one of the only POW camps in Canada that remain largely intact, it was declared a historic site instead of facing demolition. While the buildings are in ruins, as there is no maintenance or caretaking done, the structures deemed most historically important are left standing, though there are no plans to restore or protect them for the long term. While the government previously discussed the cost of restoring all or some of the buildings, the multi-million dollar price tag was too high for approval, and instead, the few remaining structures were left in a dilapidated state.

Is Camp 30 Haunted?

It's unclear whether the buildings are considered haunted, as it's difficult to find any reports from visitors to the site. The nature of Camp 30's history, as one of the only POW camps in Canada, out of forty, to imprison high-ranking German officers during WWII. Before converting the site to a POW camp, many residents were opposed to the idea of having captured Germany soldiers within a short distance of their community.

Today, the site receives many visitors, especially curious urban explorers and people intrigued by the region's history. The worn buildings, which are unstable and covered in graffiti, offer a glimpse into a dark past. While there aren't any reports of hauntings or urban legends directly associated with Camp 30, I've read that some people have heard the sound of distant bells or clinging when they visit the site. There is a nearby railroad crossing, nestled in between farmland and a one-lane road, which may explain the sound of bells.

Camp 30 sits on the border of a quiet, rural area, where slight noise can be attributed to the site, even if it's further away. Despite the lack of reporting hauntings, this site offers an eerie vibe if visited at night, especially if you're brave enough to peer into the building's openings or step inside. Like many abandoned structures, they spark many visitors' interests, though they are not maintained at all and are considered unsafe to enter or explore.

Our Visit to Camp 30

We visited the Bowmanville POW Camp, often referred to as Camp 30, in May 2022. It was a fascinating experience to view the remnants of this site, and consider the historical significant of the buildings and their occupants over the past century. While we didn't find any unusual phenomena in and around the site, we peered into several of the buildings, carefully, to take pictures, though we avoided entering inside, due to their unstable nature.

15.
The Elgin and Wintergarden Theatre (Toronto, Ontario)

The Elgin Theatre's interior, July 2018 (D. Schneider-Gagné)

The Elgin and Wintergarden Theatre, a treasured, heritage site in downtown Toronto, is one of the few surviving "double-decker" theatres in the world, and the only one of it kinds built in Canada. Famous for its Thomas Lamb design, the Elgin theatre is located on the main level, while the Wintergarden is situated on top, or the upper level of the building. This unique design served a practical purpose, as Yonge Street, where the theatre is located, was expensive, and acquiring more space in this area would greatly increase the costs. Building one theatre on top of the other, especially in a narrow space, allowed the building to feature more than one play, concert, screening, or live act at a time.

A Glimpse of the 1930s and Vaudeville

The Elgin and Wintergarden Theatre represents one of few or the only, stacked structures that have survived to the present day. With its unique vaudeville artifacts, Edwardian architecture, and 1930s theme, it's a masterpiece that includes some unusual installations and one-of-a-kind features, such as a set of old chairs from the Biograph Theatre in Chicago from the 1930s, which were installed in the Wintergarden Theatre in the 1980s. While the interior of the theatre has undergone a lot of restoration, the current designs were maintained to resemble the original era, including the manually-operated elevators and staircases, which lead to the Wintergarden, situated seven stories above the Elgin Theatre.

When the theatre opened in 1913, it was originally called Loew's Yonge Street Theatre, after Marcus Loew, the owner of the "Loew's Vaudeville Theatre" chain. It's one of the most unique historic sites in Toronto, with impressive performances, events, and ghost stories.

The Unique History and Design of the Double-Decker Yonge Street Theatre

There are many striking features to admire when visiting the Elgin and Wintergarden Theatre, whether you enjoy a tour of this beautiful space, a live performance, or a film festival screening. The vivid crimson color, gold and brass tones, and Edwardian designs featuring pillars, rich carpeting, and draperies that are immediately eye-catching. The Elgin Theatre offers a high, dome-shaped ceiling, suspended by a set of steel rods, from the Wintergarden Theatre theatre above.

The Wintergarden Theatre is accessible by a manually operated passenger elevator or a spiral staircase. While the Elgin is large, accommodating a significant audience, the upper-level theatre space is smaller and more intimate, with intricate decor including hand-crafted leaves, branches, garlands, ribbons, vintage lanterns, and other details, totaling over five thousand branches, ivy, and beech leaves. In contrast with the Elgin, the Wintergarden's theme is an enchanted forest, complete with murals of gardens, flowers, and ivy. The sound board of the theatre offers a beautiful mural of a blue sky with white clouds, greenery, and mountains.

During the original construction of the Elgin and Wintergarden Theatre, over five hundred artifacts were discovered, which essentially became an archaeological excavation. Over sixty glass and ceramic vessels were also found. As the building aged, the Ontario Heritage Trust completed a major project to restore the double theatre to its original beauty, which was designed by Mandel Sprachman, an architect. During the restoration process, the theatre space was expanded to include an additional 65,000 square feet.

The smaller theatre often featured premium performances, which were typically more expensive, much like the VIP section of today's cinemas.

It was considered a place where elite patrons would enjoy live theatre, while the more economical seats and shows were featured in the Elgin. The building's lobby contains some of the original flooring, and there is an impressive collection of well-preserved projection equipment and photographs of the theatre in its early years.

One of the greatest advantages of the Elgin and Wintergarden theatre is its location. It offers an entrance facing Yonge Street in downtown Toronto and a historic box office outside the exterior doors. It's ideally situated in the city's downtown, within walking distance of the Eaton Center, a multi-level shopping center, dining, and tourist attractions. Since its opening in the 1930s, the iconic double theatre was a prominent feature in the commercial district of Toronto and remains an essential venue for film and theatre today. In addition to featuring many top productions, the Elgin and the Wintergarden have also screened films as part of the Toronto International Film Festival (TIFF).

Wintergarden Theatre's interior, which is situated one floor above the Elgin Theatre, July 2018 (D. Schneider-Gagné)

The Chicago Connection

During the 1980s, when the theatre was undergoing a restoration, a significant amount of effort was put into maintaining its historical accuracy. In keeping with its original appearance, they purchased theatre seats from the Biograph Theatre in Chicago, which were shipped to Toronto and installed in the Elgin. When one of the seats was noticeably different in fabric colour, the theater in Chicago was contacted to inquire why it had been changed.

In what later became a popular story about the theatre, the Elgin and Wintergarden staff learned that the infamous John Dillinger, an American gangster from the 1930s, last occupied this seat. He was shot and killed as he exited the Biograph Theatre on July 22, 1934, in the late evening. The odd-coloured seat was re-upholstered to match the remaining vintage seats so they would blend into the rest of the seats in the Elgin. Today, if you visit the theatre, there is a chance that you could be seated in the last chair John Dillinger occupied before his death.

Hauntings in the Elgin and Wintergarden Theatre

While the Elgin and Wintergarden Theatre is famous for its legacy in performance arts, it's also widely popular as a haunted site, with many reports of paranormal experiences. Many stagehand workers and staff around the theatre have noticed unusual activity. One worker noticed a row of seats unfold, one at a time, as if a row of chairs were folded down to seat an invisible audience, only to quickly fold back up as if nothing happened.

The manually-operated elevators are known to unexpectedly run on their own, moving from one floor to another for no reason and without an operator inside. Many individuals who have worked in the theatre have either reported this activity, or know someone personally who witnessed the hand-operated elevators going up and down, without anyone present. Volunteers, performers, theatre employees, and guests to the Elgin and Wintergarden theatres have reported numerous supernatural occurrences throughout the venue, from the lobby and washrooms to the seating areas, stage, and elevators.

An apparition of a woman dressed in clothing from the early 1900s has often appeared in the lobby, lingering just long enough for several people to notice her presence before she suddenly disappears. While her identity is unknown, her Edwardian-style clothing may indicate that she was associated with the theatre during its early years, shortly after opening in 1913. Many paranormal investigators and groups have conducted seances and sessions using the Ouija board. During one such event, it was reported that a group made contact with a trombone player, Samuel, who tragically fell to his death in the orchestra pit in 1918.

Sharing Ghost Stories and Visiting the Theatre

We've visited the Elgin and Wintergarden Theater several times to enjoy live performances, a film screening, and a venue tour. On each visit, we never encountered any strange phenomena, though we were aware of the venue's history of hauntings at the time. The theatre regularly offers tours of both the Elgin and the Wintergarden, showcasing its rich history throughout the past century. On occasion, private paranormal groups and investigators have rented the facility to explore the supernatural side of the theater.

Between 2004 and 2005, I worked for an organization where I frequently interacted with individuals who worked in the entertainment industry, including a few former staff members and contractors who worked inside the Elgin and Wintergarden theatres. During a lunch break, the topic of haunted places in Toronto found its way into a conversation, leading to an interesting discussion of ghost stories and experiences within the theatre. There were many sightings of a lady wandering the washrooms and lobby area, with unusual sounds and moving objects occurring without reason.

I discovered many other haunting stories through casual conversations and numerous reports posted online. A man who appears to wear a brown coat is sometimes seen wandering in and around the stage. It is believed that his name is Stan and that he fell from the stage, or mezzanine, to his death in the 1980s. Reports of his sighting mention that he doesn't interact with anyone, causing loud noises or frightening occurrences, but instead disappears if anyone approaches him. Contractors working in various areas of the theatre, particularly on or near the stage, have reported seeing tools and other objects suddenly fly off of a table through the air without anyone remotely close to these items. Folded seats were seen unfolding and remaining in this position, one at a time, beginning from one end of the row to the end as if occupied by invisible spectators.

The most famous ghost in the Elgin and Wintergarden theatre is known as the Lavender Lady. She is among the most reported apparitions and often wanders towards the bathrooms or elevators. When she appears, the scent of lavender accompanies her, and she often seems confused, either stumbling as she walks or with a bit of a disheveled look. At first glance, she may seem like an ordinary person in need of help, though anytime she is approached, she disappears behind a corridor, inside the elevator, or in plain sight. Some people think this woman may have been an actress from an earlier time, and since her passing, she refuses to leave the theatre.

The origin of these ghosts and many of the stories from the Elgin and Wintergarden Theatre are not all easily traced to specific people from the past. From the last seat that John Dillinger took to the tragic deaths of Stan and Samuel, other tales may explain the more intense activity around the washroom, lobby, and elevator. In one story, it is believed that a woman was stabbed to death near the elevator on the fifth floor, where her bloodied body was discovered. Another tale alleges that a young boy fell from one of the box seats to his death and that near the second floor, he can be seen rushing by, running up or down the stairs, as if to return to where he originally met his tragic fate. A man, who is believed to be a former technician, often appears near the women's washroom on the second floor.

Several sightings have been noticed in and around the coat check room, a spot where actors could quickly change into their costumes if they were rushing to get ready for their part and didn't have sufficient time to reach the changerooms backstage. Over the years, many patrons, employees, contractors, and guests have experienced unexplainable sightings and unusual activity, which makes the double theatre unique in that it's one of, if not the most haunted live theatre in the city.

16.

The Old Don Jail (Toronto, Ontario)

———

The Don Jail, in its original state in May 2009, prior to being renovated (D. Schneider-Gagné)

The Don Jail, located at 550 Gerrard Street East, near Broadview Avenue in Toronto, housed many of the city's infamous criminals. For over a century, the iconic jail was known for its numerous escape attempts, notorious inmates, and executions. Over a century, the prison became known for its brutal treatment of inmates and the dire living conditions before its closing in 1977.

The building remained closed for approximately thirty years, used only for film productions and as a storage space, until its reopening for tours in 2009. Today, the historic building is completely renovated while maintaining its original exterior as an administration building for the Hennick Bridgepoint Hospital.

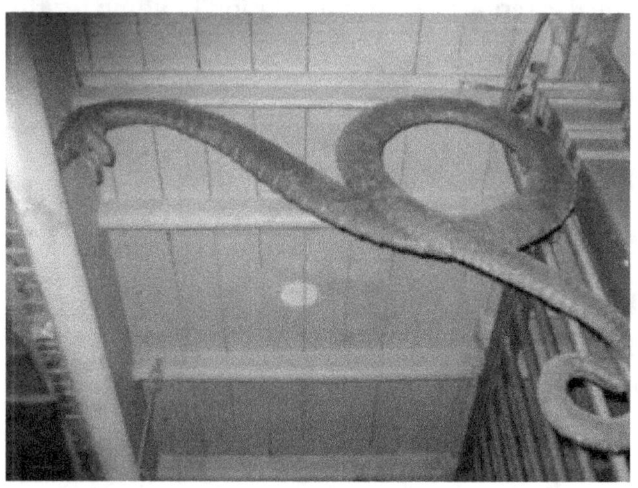

Interior details and decor of the Don Jail, Toronto, 2009 (D. Schneider-Gagné)

The History of the "Don"

In 1856, the land where the historic building sits today was purchased by the City of Toronto by the Scadding family. At the time, some of the property was situated just outside the city's limits, making it an ideal spot for a few structures: a hospice, a farm, and a prison. William Thomas, the lead architect, designed the jail in a way that was similar to the Renaissance Revival style. He was also responsible for creating several other well-known structures in the city, including St. Lawrence Hall and St. Michael's Cathedral Basilica.

While the initial start to the building of the Don Jail was promising, there were delays due to two major events: the untimely death of William Thomas and a fire that occurred in 1860 and 1862, respectively. It took five years to build, and the jail opened in 1864. The fourth jail in Toronto, the "Don," as it was often referred to, was an impressive, foreboding brick structure, with high walls extending up to 18 meters high in the yard and small cells that provided only one by three meters, or three by ten feet of space. When the building was completed in 1864, it was considered the largest of its kind in North America.

The interior rotunda of the infamous Don Jail, Toronto, 2009 (D. Schneider-Gagné)

Today, the infamous site is an administration building for Hennick Bridgepoint Active Healthcare, a facility that provides short and long-term care to residents. While twenty percent of the interior and most of the building's exterior remains restored to its original design, the 7,100 square-meter (approximately 23,200 feet) interior was completely renovated into offices. The magnitude of this project presented many challenges, which included the gutting and transforming of unstable flooring, secluded areas, cell rows, the gallows, and a rotunda-style lobby, to create a bright, open space, while preserving the heritage of the site.

The result is a fusion between the century-old limestone and brick walls of a histortical prison with modern, progressive facilities, which was recognized in 2016 with the Built Heritage Award of Excellence.

Items on display during the Doors Open tour inside the Don Jail, Toronto, 2009 (D. Schneider-Gagné)

A Dangerous, Brutal, and Tragic Legacy

The infamous Old Don jail was known for its dangerous, sometimes fatal conditions, which often had a detrimental impact on inmates with a history of mental illness. Dire situations faced in the prison included overcrowding, where more than 650 inmates were housed in a building with a capacity of only 562. While cells were designed to accommodate two prisoners in a bunk bed, a third mattress was often added to the floor, housing a third individual, which comprised personal space.

In the 1930s, the inhumane conditions in the Don jail were considered so brutal that every day served in the prison was counted as three. Overcrowding and unsanitary conditions were expected to be temporary, though they lasted three months or longer. The dire interior of the jail was so vile that prison guards, activists, and even politicians condemned the conditions. While it was initially perceived that the mayor of Toronto, at the time, would be impressed with the punitive measures taken against inmates, the reaction was disgust following a tour of the prison. Not only were inmates neglected and mistreated, but many prisoners were seriously injured, and some even killed, due to a lack of safety and security on the premises.

As some people favored harsh punishments against prisoners, there was a growing shift toward rehabilitation and ethical treatment, as many of those serving time would eventually be released, with the expectation they would re-integrate into society. The harshness of the Don jail, whether inmates served a shorter sentence awaiting transfer to a larger facility, a longer sentence, or awaiting execution, reflected the nightmarish, outdated prison life that focused more on taking punitive actions than corrective measures. A total of thirty-four executions, all by hanging, occurred at the Don Jail. These took place between 1908 and 1962, before the abolishment of the death penalty in Canada in 1967.

When the original jail was closed in 1977, it was replaced by a newer building, the "east wing," which, unfortunately, fell into dismal conditions. The loud shouting of prisoners, the vile stink of unsanitary cells, unflushable toilets, the pounding against steel bars, and ongoing fights created a chaotic environment. Furthermore, the cells were overrun with vermin, including mice and cockroaches, quickly spreading diseases. The dangerous living conditions in the prison led to its final closure in 2013, while the older, original prison remained closed for nearly thirty years before reopening for tours.

Dark corridors of the Don Jail, Toronto, 2009 (D. Schneider-Gagné)

The Notorious and the Infamous

The Boyd Gang, an infamous gang of criminals in Toronto, was highly publicized in the media for its many gun fights, bank robberies, police chases, risky captures, and jailbreaks. They were notorious for their high-profile status in Toronto, relationships with women, and pulling sensational moves for front-page news. The gang was named after Edwin Boyd, who had attempted to escape the Don, along with Willie Jackson, in 1952.

Two other members, Lennie Jackson and Steve Suchan, were caught a short distance from the prison. Steve shot one of the officers, who later died, but all four men were returned to the Don. Lennie and Steve were later hanged in the jail in 1952, standing back-to-back, as they were hanged when the trapdoors opened beneath them. While Edwin received a life sentence and Willie thirty years, they were both released in the same year, in 1966. Before his death, Edwin Boyd confessed to murder, which was not included in the numerous charges he was convicted of decades earlier.

The Ghosts of the Don

Considering the critical history and events that occurred inside the walls of the notorious Don Jail, many spirits and ghosts are believed to lurk inside as if they are trapped in time or a realm caught between here and another dimension. Following the prison's reopening in 2009 and the redevelopment project completed in 2012, ghost tours were conducted in the Don Jail. According to reports from individuals visiting the site, mentioned on Toronto Ghosts and other websites, many people have experienced a sudden chill or cold spot inside the empty prison, heaviness in the air, or a tingling sensation with a profound sense of sadness or despair.

This strange emotional sensation was described as strong, as an exterior cloud of gloom that seems to hover and affect many who enter certain jail areas. There were interesting discoveries when there was an opportunity to enter the prison, and even during its closure. During one exploration dig inside the Don in the 1980s, fifteen human remains were discovered. While they have since been moved to the nearby St. James Cemetery, it is often believed that this discovery may have conjured up spirits that refuse to leave the site.

The renovated Don Jail, now an administrative building, and part of the Hennick Bridgepoint Hospital, February 2024 (Colleen J. Cairney)

The side view of the Don Jail, which is now part of the Hennick Bridgepoint Hospital, February 2024 (Colleen J. Cairney)

Our Visit Inside the Infamous Don Jail

When we went on a tour of the Don Jail in May 2009, I often joked about the length of the line-up that day and how we waited hours to get into a place where people spent years trying to escape, or serving their sentence! Doors Open hosted the tour, an annual event where buildings throughout Toronto and other cities in the province are open to curious locals and tourists, offering an opportunity to see many unique and historic buildings for free.

During that weekend in May, the Don Jail was reopened for the first time in nearly thirty years, which garnered a lot of attention. There was a five-hour wait before we could enter the historic prison, but we were determined to get inside and experience the dark, morbid interior of the city's most famous jail. The tours were conducted every thirty minutes, allowing a small group of visitors to explore as much of the dusty, worn prison cells, blocks, rotunda, and a display of items stored inside.

While some areas of the prison were open to roam and take in the unique detailing of the doorways and architectural designs, certain cell blocks were available for limited access due to unstable floors and the potential for unsafe conditions. Some of the corridors were dimly lit, which made it difficult to see clearly, though we managed to cover as many spaces as possible, including a few cramped, worn cells. The yard's outer wall showcased the inmates' names, who etched their autographs, and the years during which they served prison time.

Today, the old Don is transformed into an administration building for the nearby hospital, where the interior was completely gutted, with modernized offices and facilities. The preserved exterior of the famous prison is a reminder of the city's criminal history.

17.
Dundurn Castle (Hamilton, Ontario)

A path to the Dundurn Castle, Hamilton, Ontario, July 2019 (D. Schneider-Gagné)

The Dundurn Castle is a scenic, iconic estate located a short distance from the city's downtown core. It's a well-preserved heritage building that hosts numerous events year-round, from holiday festivities and guest tours to private parties, weddings, and social occasions. This national historic site, built in the 1830s, includes the gatehouse known as Battery Lodge, the gardener's cottage, the MacInnes Stable, the park pavilion, entrance gates known as Rolph Gates, and additional structures situated on a picturesque, 13-hectare park between Hamilton Harbour and Burlington Heights, called Cootes Paradise.

The History of Dundurn Castle

Richard Beasily began building the estate in 1800. It was later purchased by John Solomon Cartwright in 1832 and sold to MacNab, who transformed the property into a mansion. The location was perfect for capturing the natural beauty of the landscape, rich forest, and breathtaking views of the bay. The main house, or residence, was designed by Robert Wetherell, a local Hamilton architect. Over time, the estate was further developed to include the various buildings and structures that remain on the property today.

The extraordinary property features grassy hills, trees, ravines, slopes, and gardens that adorn the park. One of the most prominent individuals in the Dundurn, Sir Alan Napier MacNab, was an entrepreneur and politician. Its unique design evokes a sense of mysterious beauty, blending classic and Gothic Revival styles throughout the estate, with an Italianate influence throughout the main house. The entire estate was built over two years between 1834 and 1835.

Staircase inside the Dundurn Castle, July 2019 (D. Schneider-Gagné)

Before residing in the nineteenth century castle, McNab married Elizabeth Brooke, who died in November 1826, due to childbirth complications. He married his second wife, Mary, who died in May of 1846, of tuberculosis. She was the daughter of the Johnstown District Sheriff, John Stuart, and birthed two children.

The Dundurn Castle, July 2019 (D. Schneider-Gagné)

Famous Site for Television and Film

Does the Gothic mansion appear familiar? Dundurn Castle has been featured in many well-known film productions, including Crimson Peak, the Umbrella Academy, Murdoch Mysteries, Sort Of (a series from HBO), and The Good Witch. It's the ideal setting for a Victorian-era film, a gothic romance, or even a classic horror.

Is the Dundurn Castle Haunted?

At first glance, the iconic mansion doesn't initially conjure thoughts of hauntings or reports of the paranormal. This postcard-perfect city landmark is often associated with interesting tours of Victorian-style decor, numerous rooms, and guides who wear period clothing and are well-versed in the castle's history. The residence is most notably introduced as the home of Sir Allan MacNab, known as the premier between 1854 and 1856 in pre-Confederation Canada.

There is also a dark, bloody past that haunts the estate and a history of violence that plagues the property to the present day. The grounds surrounding the castle have a violent and bloody history, where eleven men were hung for treason across the street in 1813. Cholera victims were also transported to plague sheds near the property, where they were left to die.

Many visitors to the castle have reported disembodied voices and singing travelling throughout the main house. Just outside the bedroom of MacNab's late wife, Mary, is where people experience cold chills or a sudden draft, even when the rest of the castle is set to a warm, cozy temperature without the hint of a breeze. Sir Allan MacNab and his family may remain in ghostly form within the castle.

Our Visit to Dundurn Castle

We visited the Dundurn Castle for a tour in July 2019. It was an interesting place to explore, with seemingly infinite rooms and spaces that are well preserved from an earlier time. While we didn't experince any unusual sightings or similar occurrences, one of the gas-lit lanterns in the kitchen blew out, unexpectedly. It was strange, as the remaining row of lights appeared untouched. While ghost stories were not mentioned or included in the tour, we did keep an eye out, just in case anything struck us as bizarre or unexpected.

18.

Century Manor (Hamilton, Ontario)

The front of the Century Manor, April 2024 (D. Schneider-Gagné)

The old mansion on the hill, Century Manor, represents a significant part of Hamilton's psychiatric history and the site of a dark, haunting presence. It's an impressive, gothic structure built in a Victorian style and originally called East House. Surrounded by a spacious parcel of land, just over five hundred acres, the building is located just off of West 5th Street. It's a unique structure that many consider one of the city's most prominent historic buildings, which should be preserved and protected as a heritage site.

The History of the Hamilton Psychiatric Hospital

Front exterior of the Century Manor, facing the street, April 2024 (D. Schneider-Gagné)

East House, as it was originally called, was built in the late 1880s and opened in 1884. It was the main structure in a series of buildings that were in use for nearly one hundred years until the 1980s. Originally, the city built its first psychiatric facility in the late 1800s, the Hamilton Asylum for the Insane, which was later renated the Ontario Hospital and then the Hamilton Psychiatric Hospital.

The institution opened in 1876 and offered accommodations for up to two hundred patients, with over five hundred acres of land consisting of a farm, services, and shops to create a self-sufficient community. Initially, the Barton Building, under the direction of Dr. R. Burke, was opened to provide a more humane approach to the treatment of people suffering from mental illnesses. Due to its popularity and proximity to a growing population, it expanded to meet the needs of Ontarians, as there were only two other psychiatric hospitals in Toronto and London at that time.

The isolated nature of the psychiatric facility, only accessible through a dirt road, required self-sufficiency. As the hospital expanded into the 1900s, several shops, including a fire hall, upholstery and sewing service, on-site tailor, chapel, butcher, greenhouse, bakery, cellar, and a farm complete with cattle, pigs, chickens, fruits, and vegetables. There were recreational facilities, such as tennis courts and bowling greens, as well as a rink for ice skating and curling. Vehicles ready for transport were always available, making it easier to shuttle patients needing urgent care or specialized treatment to another hospital.

In the 1890s, the hospital became famous for its new, humane treatments and practices for mental illnesses. At that time, there were over a hundred patients and close to one hundred and twenty staff. There were regular events to raise funds, including the annual Asylum Ball, which attracted the local elite and famous of Hamilton. As the facility quickly expanded, the number of patients grew to twelve hundred in 1909. In 1929, it was recognized as one of the province's best institutions for advanced mental health treatments.

Throughout the mid-1900s, the hospital continued to thrive. However, some of the land had to be auctioned off, leaving just over eighty acres of farmland and recreational space, which provided therapeutic benefits to patients. The hospital was renamed the Hamilton

Psychiatric Hospital in 1968 and offered treatment for several conditions, including addiction, mental health for teenagers and young adults, and forensic psychiatry.

In the decades following, many buildings were demolished, and the land's ownership was transferred to the province. Initially built in 1884, the East House, which is known today as the Century Manor, briefly became a museum after the treatment facilities ceased, until its permanent closure in 1995. Today, Century Manor remains fully intact and is one of three surviving buildings on the site. It's located on a thirty-acre parcel of land directly across from a Mohawk College campus on Fennel Avenue.

An Uncertain Future

The front entrance to the Century Manor, April 2024 (D. Schneider-Gagné)

Since its permanent closure in 1995, following its unsuccessful transformation into a museum for a short time, the Century Manor remains closed and left to decay. While several proposals suggest a revitalization of the site, including selling the land to the college and allocating the funds to build affordable housing in Hamilton's downtown core in 2018, this plan didn't materialize following a change in government. In 2020, the province designated the area for a new long-term care site with a ministerial zoning order or MZO, including a high-rise with approximately eighteen stories.

Currently, the property remains in trust through the province of Ontario. However, there is an ongoing debate about whether the property can be sold for private development or other purposes that do not align with the public's best interests. There is a continued interest in developing the site for Mohawk College through an agreement or partnership. While other options are considered, there is a growing division about Century Manor's future. As of 2024, the property is in the care of a private commercial real estate company, and its future is unknown. Should this abandoned site of historic significance be demolished to make room for modern infrastructure or preserved as a heritage property?

Scary Stories from the Abandoned Asylum

One of the exterior walls of the Century Manor, April 2024 (D. Schneider-Gagné)

While the Century Manor remains permanently closed, previous visitors and urban explorers to the site have reported eerie, chilling occurrences inside the walls of the abandoned asylum. Many stories I've encountered were posted on various websites and forums detailing individual experiences at the Manor. In one incident, a small group of men who set out to explore the building clearly heard the bone-chilling screams of a woman. A search of the premises confirmed the structure was empty, with no one inside and no one outside.

The abandoned structure is commonly referred to as haunted, and there are cautionary stories and warnings not to enter alone or remain inside for long periods of time. A wide range of experiences were reported over the years, from nothing unusual at all to an unexpected tug on clothing, a physical tap or push, to more unnerving sounds, and the moving of objects. During a photoshoot in one of the rooms on the main floor, the crew was interrupted by the sounds of dragging upstairs.

When they investigated the second floor, they found a steel bedpan in the hallway. When the dragging sound resumed moments later, further inspection led to the same steel bedpan, which had been moved from its original spot, with no one in sight. Security guards have expressed their unease about entering the building, as several encounters included being shoved or pushed by an invisible force and an uncomfortable presence.

One of the scariest stories reported inside the old "East House" or Century Manor was recalled by a security guard working on the site one evening. During patrols of the building, he encountered an underground tunnel system, which led him through a series of abandoned corridors, where he stumbled across a dead end to one with a wooden door. This piqued his curiosity when he heard voices coming from the other side of the door. Taking a moment to compose himself, he opened the door to find two women wearing nurse uniforms. They appeared to be old-fashioned, as if they were from the early part of the 1900s. As they slowly turned to face the security guard, one of them spoke, "See, I told you he would find us."

The unbelievable discovery caused the security guard to quickly leave the room and slam the door. Shaking, he took a moment to calm his nerves, as the startling sight of two nurses from another era must have been difficult to process. Then, as he remained in the dark hallway for a few minutes, he turned to face the wooden door and decided it was worth a second look. Upon entering a second time, he found the room completely empty, with no signs of use. He also noted there were no exits or means to leave the room, which meant the nurses were either apparitions, a doorway into the past, or a figment of his imagination.

While the Manor has been closed and no entry is permitted, one of the underground tunnels is connected to a local restaurant and pub, "The Cellar," which is accessible through the neighboring Mohawk College campus. The popular spot is decorated with turn-of-the-century brickwork and vaulted ceilings, with a theme similar to that of the abandoned hospital.

A Film and Reports on the Century Manor

The popularity of this site inspired a local documentary produced by film students at Sheridan College, "The Hauntings of Century Manor." The film included interviews with individuals who have entered the asylum and their first-hand accounts of unusual events inside the hospital's walls. Details of the film production are included on the International Movie Database website (IMDB) and the Sheridan College BFTV Channel website.

My Visit to the Century Manor

I spent the day in Hamilton to enjoy a bit of urban hiking in the area before heading towards the abandoned Century Manor. The site is accessible by a paved road between modern buildings around 5th West Street and Fennel Avenue West. I walked from a road off of 5th West, which led directly to Century Manor. It was completely sealed off, including boarded doors and windows, so entering the structure would be tricky. During my visit, I noticed several vehicles slow down, maybe to look at the building or patrol the area.

There is a stark contrast between the Mohawk College campus, the newer public buildings, and the historic structure that offers a peek into the sometimes dark past of psychiatry. While my visit was limited to observing the exterior of the asylum, I took my time, imagining what it would have been like over a century ago. The impressive building appeared to be the ideal setting for a horror film or psychological thriller.

19.

Kirby Road (Vaughan, Ontario)

An abandoned bridge on the closed portion of Kirby Road, Vaughan, Ontario, May 2024 (D. Schneider-Gagné)

Kirby Road is one of the unexpected places I discovered when I wrote this book. As I neared the last few chapters, I asked for feedback and suggestions for unusual sites and haunted places. While there are seemingly infinite sites throughout Ontario to explore, I was looking for new ideas, something lesser known. I was curious what other people would come up with, especially hidden spots in Southern Ontario. Kirby Road immediately intrigued me, as it initially reminded me of Old Finch Avenue, another notoriously haunted road in Scarborough.

From Bolton and Kleinburg to Vaughan

At first glance, Kirby Road appears like any other road on the outskirts of Vaughan and Brampton. It's easily accessible by car, and depending on which part of the road you access, it's a moderate hike from the closest transit station. Kirby Avenue starts in the west, at Albion Vaughan Road, just above where this road crosses Highway 50, close to Bolton and Brampton.

It extends east towards Dufferin Street, just north of Vaughan, close to Richmond Hill. While a significant portion of the road is accessible, running straight from east to west in the York Region, a small part of Kirby Road is closed as part of the Humber Valley Heritage Trail, which runs off of Huntington Road. It's protected as a heritage site and part of the Nashville Conservation Preserve. This path is inaccessible by car, though it's easily hikable, and it includes an abandoned bridge just a few steps from Huntington Road.

While the portion of Kirby Road between Dufferin and Bathurst Streets in Vaughan is scheduled for an extension, the older, run-down portion, which is now closed, is part of a conservation area and a hiking trail. The extension project is expected to be completed by the summer of 2026. Kirby Road is an integral part of the transportation that helps residents commute as the area quickly expands with an influx of urban growth.

The Legend and Haunting of Selina

The urban legend of Kirby Road is considered by many to be one of the most famous in the Peel Region. The most well-known haunting of the road is based on the spirit of a girl named Selina, who was killed in an accident. According to the local urban legend, Selina's spirit lingers, sometimes appearing in a tree by the side of the road or wandering by her gravestone, which has since been removed. The gravestone allegedly had her name carved in cursive writing. There was no last name, just "Selina," accented with a heart and the words inscribed, "I'm a cute kid."

Kirby Road sign, where the road is closed, Vaughan, Ontario in May 2024 (D. Schneider-Gagné)

According to what appears to be old newspaper clippings and records of Selina's tragic death, a car accident occurred on November 1, 1993, near the intersection of Pine Valley Drive and Kirby Road. There were four occupants in the car, which included Selina Degasperis, who died in the accident, and her friend and sister, both of whom were injured. Many visitors to the area, precisely where the tragedy occurred, experience tapping on the windows of their car or the sound of a girl yelling in the distance. Other sightings include a young girl under a nearby tree, close to the gravestone, or where it once stood.

Closed off area on Kirby Road, May 2024 (D. Schneider-Gagné)

The gravestone with the unusual cursive signature, left as a memorial to Selina, was removed due to concerns that it may attract vandalism. Some believe the memorial would summon her spirit and that removing it meant she would move on and no longer remain "stuck" on Kirby Road. There has been speculation as to whether Selina's death was an accident or if she was killed on purpose. This stems from a story about Selina's father, who was believed to be part of a gang who disapproved of Selina's boyfriend. Some tales of Selina's death involve her father, and there have been reports of Selina's anger towards her father remaining as a dark presence. Some thought that removing the gravestone would bring a sense of peace to her spirit.

A Film About Kirby Road

While there are blog posts and articles about the urban legend of Selina Degasperis, including photos of newspaper clippings, some people dispute the authenticity of her existence, let alone her death, and whether or not the entire story was fabricated to create an urban legend. A film shot in and around Toronto, "The Haunted House of Kirby Road," is unrelated, though often associated with this particular Kirby Road. The movie was filmed in the fall of 2016, and it ignited a renewed interest in the haunted road, resulting in more visits and paranormal investigations of the area.

Abandoned bridge on Kirby Road, the closed section, part of Humber Valley Heritage Trail, May 2024 (D. Schneider-Gagné)

The "Hell House" Story

At least two other stories originate from Kirby Road, associated with hauntings around the area. One common story is linked to Selina's father, who was allegedly part of a violent, gang that regularly met in a local barn next to a farmhouse called a "hell house." According to the urban legend, the man (sometimes believed to be Selina's father) who lived on the farm lost his mind and became so unhinged that he murdered his entire family. Some stories mention the man as Selina's father and how his anger and disapproval of her interracial relationship with a young man led to his violent behavior and then murder.

While the reason for the tragic killings is often debated, the entire story, including the man responsible for the murder, is questionable, as there is no evidence to support it. The barn, considered the location of the "hell house," was frequented by trespassers and has since been demolished.

The Pickup Truck Story

Another story that's been shared online about Kirby Road is a semi-truck or pickup truck with one headlight. It's been reported that this truck will suddenly appear and pass under the bridge of Kirby Road. According to curious visitors and investigators who visit the road, the semi-truck will drive past people and their vehicles to scare them away so they will leave. While it's unclear who the truck's driver is, it's believed they do not welcome guests to the road and will appear unexpectedly, usually at night. There are a variety of reports online, including claims that the truck was caught on video, though the story's validity still needs to be verified.

My Visit to Kirby Road

When I initially searched Kirby Road online, I noticed that a significant portion of it was scheduled to be developed, which made it a bit challenging to find the origin of the urban legend and related hauntings. One area that struck me as fascinating was the closed portion of the road and an abandoned bridge over the Humber River, which is not part of a heritage trail. I soon learned that some of the reports of unusual activity were allegedly from or near this region. It's an ideal area for hiking, and it's easily found off Huntington Road, which leads to the Nashville Conservation Preserve on the outskirts of Vaughan, near Bolton and Kleinburg, and just east of Brampton.

The scenic trail led me through a path overgrown with greenery, crossing over the McEwen bridge, which includes a sign warning of its unsafe condition. It took just a few minutes to locate the bridge directly on the trail, which leads further into a natural forested area. While I didn't notice anything strange, it's clear that the area is protected, and the bridge is considered to have heritage significance. The stories of hauntings and unusual experiences are often reported to occur in the late evening or at night.

20.
Lower Bay Subway Station (Toronto, Ontario)

Photo of the abandoned "lower" Bay Station beneath the regular Bay platform, May 2019 (D. Schneider-Gagné)

If you live in or around Toronto or visit the city often, you're likely familiar with the TTC (Toronto Transit Commission) and the subway system. The two main subway lines consist of the Yonge-University line, which runs in a U-shape from Finch and Yonge, south to Union Station, and north on the other side, towards Vaughan. Crossing two stations on the Yonge-University line (St. George and Yonge) is the Bloor line, which extends from Kennedy Station in the east

(Scarborough) to Kipling in the west (Etobicoke). Between the Yonge and St. George stations is Bay Station, a busy hub for weekday commuters and visitors to the city's core, where you'll find numerous attractions, including the AGO (Art Gallery of Ontario) and ROM (Royal Ontario Museum).

The History of the Abandoned Subway Station

While the Bay subway station doesn't stand out as a particularly unique depot for locals and tourists, a lesser-known station called the Lower Bay subway station lurks beneath. This abandoned station was originally built in the 1960s to create an intersecting route beneath four sets of tracks and three routes, though today, the station has two platforms, serving trains travelling east and west on one route.

Once it was determined that the lower level station beneath the current Bay station was constructed in error, it was ended and quickly closed to the public in September 1966. Not only was the lower station inefficient, it became a source of confusion and often caused delays, which impacted the subway system. It's now referred to as "Lower Bay" and is rarely open to the public for tours and curious urban explorers.

Subway cars on display during an exhibit of the "lower" Bay station, May 2019 (D. Schneider-Gagné)

A Popular Filming Location

Despite the current dormant state of the "ghost" subway station, there are plenty of reasons to access this space. TTC employees use the lower level for training purposes, and a number of famous films and television series have featured the abandoned train tunnel in many scenes. This hidden gem has been featured in The Handmaid's Tale, Repo Man, Suicide Squad, Resident Evil, Shazam!, Total Recall, and many other series and films. The empty, unadorned platform is an ideal setting for many scenes and, in my opinion, would be the perfect spot for a horror film!

Apparitions and Hauntings in the "Lower Bay" Station

Since the lower subway station was abandoned, it has been primarily used as a storage space for equipment. While it's closed to the public, a limited number of people, including film crew and transit employees, access this area. Staff have reported seeing the apparition of a woman or human-like figure wandering inside the tunnels. The most common sighting is a woman dressed in red, which is strikingly odd, as only authorized individuals have access to the lower subway station. She's often spotted roaming close to the entrance and exit areas of the closed station.

When the lady or ghost is described in detail, she is seen wearing a long, red dress, but her legs and feet are missing, which creates the illusion that she's floating around the subway platform and tunnel. The lady in the red dress, as she's commonly known, usually appears for thirty seconds, then disappears, unexpectedly, in thin air. Workers who encounter the apparition leave the tunnel quickly after the sighting, and in some cases, refuse to re-enter the abandoned station. While a handful of people have spotted the ghost firsthand, most transit employees have at least heard of her.

In some reports, a singing voice can be heard in the tunnel, often attributed to ghost of the woman, even if she isn't visibly seen. There isn't any specific time or location where she appears, so the sightings are random and unexpected. The origin of her presence is unknown, and no other apparitions or hauntings have been as widely reported as the lady in the red dress. To this day, she remains a mysterious urban legend without a background story, though she may inspire a filmmaker to create one someday!

Our Visit to the Old Subway Station

The popular stories of the haunted subway tunnel have created a broad interest in the station, which has been opened more frequently to the public to educate people on the history of the city's transit system, with family-friendly activities and displays. Halloween festivals in the Lower Bay station are also growing in popularity, with many families and enthusiasts of the site lining up to investigate the abandoned tunnel.

We enjoyed a visit to the site in 2019, during Doors Open in Toronto, one of our favourite ways to explore the unique and interesting side of the city. The doorway to the secret layer below the current Bay station was opened to reveal what appeared to be another version of it, only dimmer and worn down. The abandoned station was decorated with displays of the model subway trains on the platform and large posters featuring the movies filmed there. While the tunnels were off-limits, we could walk through some empty, older train cars, learn about the station, and peek at the mysterious underground, where the lady in red floats aimlessly through the darkness.

Discovering and Exploring Unique Places

Since the summer of 2020, when I began working on this book, I learned of the many ghost towns and unique sites across Ontario. There are hundreds, possibly close to a thousand, which have become more well-known through urban explorers who discover them, or a hidden gem that has yet to be found. The handful of sites I've visited so far have inspired me to look for new, unfamiliar places, while also looking back through old photographs of places I've seen before.

My fascination of ghost stories and urban legends inspired me to write about and share my experiences, which quickly became a passion project. It's my goal to explore more abandoned, historic, and haunted sites throughout Ontario and beyond. I'm working on a follow-up to this book, where I'll have more photos, research, and spooky stories. I hope this book inspires you to get in touch with your sense of adventure, too!

References

Screaming Tunnel | Niagara Falls Public Library. (n.d.). https://my.nflibrary.ca/HistoricNiagara/DigitalExhibits/ScreamingTunnel

Grundhauser, E. (2022, November 22). Screaming Tunnel. Atlas Obscura. https://www.atlasobscura.com/places/screaming-tunnel

Haunted Hamilton. (2017, April 12). The Screaming Tunnel | Creepy Canada (2003). YouTube. https://m.youtube.com/watch?v=_fPj4RuXL_c

Ghost Walks. (2023, January 6). Screaming Tunnel | Niagara's haunted place to visit | Articles. https://ghostwalks.com/articles/screaming-tunnel-niagara-visit

Thayer, T. (2024, March 20). Bruce Trail Conservancy. Bruce Trail Conservancy. https://brucetrail.org/

Ugc. (2024, May 26). Blue Ghost Tunnel. Atlas Obscura. https://www.atlasobscura.com/places/blue-ghost-tunnel

Hikingthegta. (2018, September 30). Merritton Tunnel (Blue Ghost Tunnel). Hiking the GTA. https://hikingthegta.com/2018/02/28/merritton-tunnel-blue-ghost-tunnel/

———

Daily Hive, Brooke Taylor (2021, October 20). There are two haunted tunnels near Toronto that you can visit. https://dailyhive.com/toronto/haunted-tunnels-near-toronto

———

Researcher, S. (n.d.). Scarborough - Old Finch Road. https://www.torontoghosts.org/index.php/the-city-of-toronto/scarborough/186-scarborough-old-finch-road-

———

Basa, E. (2022, April 9). This allegedly haunted bridge in Toronto has teenagers testing a terrifying urban legend after dark. Narcity. https://www.narcity.com/toronto/this-allegedly-haunted-bridge-in-toronto-has-teenagers-testing-a-terrifying-urban-legend-after-dark

Old Finch Avenue Bridge - HistoricBridges.org. (n.d.). https://historicbridges.org/bridges/browser/?bridgebrowser=ontario/finchtoronto/

———

Gibraltar Point Lighthouse: History & Old Pictures. (2021, July 20) https://torontopubliclibrary.typepad.com/local-history-genealogy/2021/07/gibraltar-point-lighthouse-history-old-pictures.html

———

Ghost stories still haunt Gibraltar Point Lighthouse on Toronto Islands, The Toronto Star. (2018, July 21)

https://www.thestar.com/life/travel/ghost-stories-still-haunt-gibraltar-point-lighthouse-on-toronto-islands/article_68b189e3-743d-5b52-b255-647628cd2d92.html

———

New light on Toronto's oldest cold case. (2022, November 3). 1812 and All That. https://eamonnokeeffe1812.com/gibraltarpointlighthousemurder/

———

Cooper's Falls Trail. (n.d.). https://www.gravenhurst.ca/en/explore-and-play/coopers-falls-trail.aspx

———

Five Ontario ghost towns to explore this Halloween weekend, The Toronto Star. (2022, October 29)

https://www.thestar.com/autos/2022/10/29/five-ontario-ghost-towns-to-explore-this-halloween-weekend.html

———

Toronto Stories (2008) ◈ 5.6 | Drama. (2008, September 9). IMDb. https://www.imdb.com/title/tt1113827/

———

Lucia. (2023, February 8). Encyclopaedia of the Impossible: The Cabbagetown Tunnel Monster of Toronto. The Ghost in My Machine. https://theghostinmymachine.com/2023/08/07/encyclopaedia-of-the-impossible-the-cabbagetown-tunnel-monster-of-toronto/

———

Throwback Thursday: The Tunnel Monster of Cabbagetown – Cabbagetown Residents Association – CRA. (n.d.). https://cabbagetowner.com/tbt-tunnel-monster-of-cabbagetown/

———

Researcher, S. (n.d.-a). Preston - an old hotel. https://www.torontoghosts.org/index.php/the-province-of-ontario/south-western/354-preston-an-old-hotel-

Tracing the decline of the Preston Springs hotel from an iconic landmark to a dangerous eyesore, James Jackson, Record Reporter, Waterloo Region Record, (2020, January 23).

https://www.therecord.com/news/waterloo-region/2020/01/23/tracing-the-decline-of-the-preston-springs-hotel-from-an-iconic-landmark-to-a-dangerous-eyesore.html

———

Staff, C. (2022, August 20). LANDMARKS Preston mineral springs lost but not forgotten. CambridgeToday.ca. https://www.cambridgetoday.ca/local-news/landmarks-preston-mineral-springs-lost-but-not-forgotten-5704772

———

Banger, C., & Banger, C. (2021, January 28). After 30 years empty, an emergency order was issued to demolish the Preston Springs Hotel. Here's how it unfolded. Kitchener. https://kitchener.ctvnews.ca/after-30-years-empty-an-emergency-order-was-issued-to-demolish-the-preston-springs-hotel-here-s-how-it-unfolded-1.5286011

———

Maw, I. (2018, May 1). The Mystery of the Preston Springs Hotel - Isaac Maw - medium. Medium. https://isaacmaw.medium.com/the-mystery-of-the-preston-springs-hotel-7521161d7463

———

Exploring a historic and haunted hotel the Preston Springs Hotel | FREAKTOGRAPHY. (2022, April 7). FREAKTOGRAPHY. https://freaktography.com/exploring-a-historic-and-haunted-hotel-the-preston-springs-hotel/

Didier, M. J. (n.d.). Mackenzie House. https://www.torontoghosts.org/index.php/the-city-of-toronto/public-buildings/73-mackenzie-house

Ghosts be gone? Ancaster's haunted Hermitage gets eye catching facelift, Jon Wells Spectator Reporter, The Hamilton Spectator (2016, June 27).

https://www.thespec.com/news/hamilton-region/ghosts-be-gone-ancasters-haunted-hermitage-gets-eye-catching-facelift/article_8b611bc6-b902-5cff-b3bd-aea8cf003b1f.html

Hikingthegta. (2015, November 20). The Haunted Hermitage. Hiking the GTA. https://hikingthegta.com/2015/11/19/the-haunted-hermitage/

Hamilton Conservation Authority. (2020, July 13). Hermitage Gatehouse - Hamilton Conservation Authority. https://conservationhamilton.ca/hermitage-gatehouse/

Gagne, M. (2020, October 30). Haunted Simcoe: The Beck House. Barrie 360. https://barrie360.com/haunted-simcoe-the-beck-house/

Haunted Cemetery Road Trip: The Beck House. (2023, March 27). Cemetery Photography by Chantal Larochelle. https://chantallarochelle.ca/2022/10/16/haunted-cemetery-road-trip-the-beck-house/

Kong-Perring, S. (2022, December 13). 10 Unbelievable Facts About Beck House, Canada's Most Haunted House. TheTravel. https://www.thetravel.com/facts-about-canadas-most-haunted-house/

Carl Beck House | Penetanguishene Heritage. (n.d.). https://heritage.penetanguishene.ca/heritage-location.php?id=12

Kevin, V. a. P. B. (2021b, July 8). Newmarket Ghost Canal. Day Trip in an Hour. https://daytripinanhour.com/2020/05/23/newmarket-ghost-canal/

Hikingthegta. (2019, February 12). Newmarket Ghost Canal. Hiking the GTA. https://hikingthegta.com/2015/06/25/newmarket-ghost-canal/

———

Malabar Limited - Toronto Store. (n.d.-b). https://www.malabar.net/toronto.html

Researcher, S. (n.d.-a). Malabar costumes. https://www.torontoghosts.org/index.php/the-city-of-toronto/private-business/132-malabar-costumes-

---

Hamilton. (2022, March 28). Albion falls. Tourism Hamilton. https://tourismhamilton.com/albion-falls/

Albion Falls - city of waterfalls. (2017b, August 13). City of Waterfalls. https://www.cityofwaterfalls.ca/albion-falls/

Ghost Walks. (2023b, April 28). Albion Falls in Hamilton was Canada's Darkest Town - Dark History Article. https://ghostwalks.com/articles/albion-falls-darkest-in-canada

---

POW Camp 30 - National Trust for Canada. (2022b, March 20). National Trust for Canada. https://nationaltrustcanada.ca/nt-endangered-places/pow-camp-30

'Spirits of Camp 30' tell stories of Bowmanville's past, Parvaneh Pessian, Oshawa This Week, (2011, October 26).

https://www.durhamregion.com/life/spirits-of-camp-30-tell-stories-of-bowmanvilles-past/article_c4e2952e-8143-520e-aa57-91b03adbbe64.html

---

Ominous. (n.d.). Ominous Abandoned Places. https://ominous.app/browse/site/613

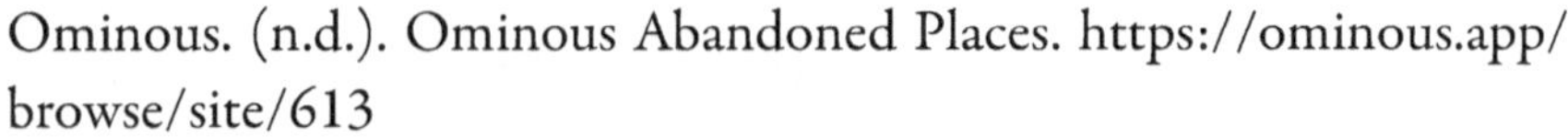

Canada, H. P. (2014, April 22). Check out the ghostly ruins of a Canadian POW camp (PHOTOS). HuffPost. https://www.huffpost.com/archive/ca/entry/check-out-the-ghostly-ruins-of-a-canadian-pow-camp-photos_n_5194091

Ontario Heritage Trust | Elgin Winter Garden Theatre Homepage. (n.d.). Ontario Heritage Trust. https://www.heritagetrust.on.ca/ewg/ewg-home

Ontario Heritage Trust | Ghost stories. (n.d.). Ontario Heritage Trust. https://www.heritagetrust.on.ca/ewg/ewg-home/learn/ghost-stories

Researcher, S. (n.d.-b). Elgin/Winter Garden Theatre(s). https://www.torontoghosts.org/index.php/the-city-of-toronto/ private-business/129-elginwinter-garden-theatres-

―――――――――

Marie, D. (2024, March 9). Old Don Jail – Toronto's Intimidating & Imposing Prison on the Hill. TorontoJourney416. https://www.torontojourney416.com/old-don-jail/

―――――――――

Hell House: Why the Don Jail is a wretched, dangerous dungeon that should have been shut down ages ago, Toronto Life, (2010, December 6). https://torontolife.com/city/hell-house/

―――――――――

Researcher, S. (n.d.-f). The Old Don Jail. https://www.torontoghosts.org/index.php/the-city-of-toronto/ public-buildings/103-the-old-don-jail-?showall=1

―――――――――

HistoricPlaces.ca - HistoricPlaces.ca. (n.d.). https://www.historicplaces.ca/en/rep-reg/ place-lieu.aspx?id=12341&pid=0

―――――――――

Local Ghosts | HPL. (n.d.). HPL. https://lha.hpl.ca/articles/ local-ghosts

―――――――――

Nykolas Moore. (2024, April 10). https://ignitenews.mohawkcollege.ca/the-mystery-of-century-manor/

The Hauntings of Century Manor (Short 2021) | Short, documentary. (2021, October 31). IMDb. https://www.imdb.com/title/tt14188178/

———

2020 - The Century Manor Hauntings. (n.d.). SHERIDAN BFTV CORE 1 DOCS. https://www.bftv-docs.com/2020—-the-century-manor-hauntings.html[1]

———

Dumbreck, S. (2022, November 28). Historic Century Manor | Haunted Hamilton | CEKAN. Cekan.ca. https://cekan.ca/hamilton/historic-century-manor-haunted-hamilton/

———

Maxwell, J. (2022, March 16). What's happening with Century Manor? Advocates say they're no closer to an answer. CBC. https://www.cbc.ca/news/canada/hamilton/century-manor-1.6379599

———

Abandoned Century Manor Insane Asylum Hamilton Ontario. (2023, January 6). FREAKTOGRAPHY. https://freaktography.com/abandoned-century-manor/

2020 - The Century Manor Hauntings. (n.d.-b). SHERIDAN BFTV CORE 1 DOCS. https://www.bftv-docs.com/2020—-the-century-manor-hauntings.html[2]

---

1. https://www.bftv-docs.com/2020---the-century-manor-hauntings.html
2. https://www.bftv-docs.com/2020---the-century-manor-hauntings.html

Kirby Road. (n.d.). Kirby Road. https://hauntedkirbyroad.home.blog/

https://www.vaughan.ca/about-city-vaughan/projects-and-initiatives/ infrastructure-engineering-and-construction-projects/kirby-road-extension

———

Staff, I., & Staff, I. (2019, May 14). 5 Urban Legends of Brampton to make your skin crawl | InBrampton. Insauga | Local Online News. https://www.insauga.com/5-urban-legends-of-brampton-to-make-your-skin-crawl/

———

Hikingthegta. (2018b, December 27). Abandoned Kirby Road. Hiking the GTA. https://hikingthegta.com/2018/04/09/abandoned-kirby-road/

———

Kirby Road Extension | City of Vaughan. (n.d.). https://www.vaughan.ca/about-city-vaughan/projects-and-initiatives/ infrastructure-engineering-and-construction-projects/kirby-road-extension

———

The Haunted House on Kirby Road (2016) ◈ 3.4 | Adventure, comedy, horror. (2016, October 14). IMDb. https://www.imdb.com/title/tt4765188/

Caspersz, K. (2023, October 19). This Toronto Haunted House Is In An Abandoned Subway Station That's Been Closed For 57 Years. Narcity. https://www.narcity.com/toronto/toronto-abandoned-subway-station-haunted-house-halloween

———

8 Popular Filming Locations in Toronto, 96.9 FM Radio Humber.ca, by Josh Welsh (n.d.)

https://radio.humber.ca/whats-happening/2021/8-popular-filming-locations-in-toronto.html

———

TTC Lower Bay Subway Station – Haunted Toronto database. (2019, January 17). Michelle McKay Paranormal. https://coldspot.org/2013/10/10/ttc-lower-bay-subway-station-haunted-ghosts-toronto-ontario-canada/

———

Landau, J. (2022, June 8). Here's what it's like inside Toronto's famous abandoned Lower Bay station. blogTO. https://www.blogto.com/city/2022/06/inside-toronto-lower-bay-station/

———

Bay lower. (n.d.). https://www.stationfixation.com/2016/12/bay-lower.html?m=1

———

The Other Side TV. (2017, April 6). How to use an EVP Recorder | The other side. https://theothersidetv.ca/ghost-hunting-resources/ghost-hunting-tips-tricks/evp-recorder/

Don't miss out!

Visit the website below and you can sign up to receive emails whenever Deborah Schneider-Gagne publishes a new book. There's no charge and no obligation.

https://books2read.com/r/B-A-IPPWB-HVIVD

BOOKS2READ

Connecting independent readers to independent writers.

9 798822 762518 2